WORDS AROUND THE TABLE

by
GAIL RAMSHAW

Art by
LINDA EKSTROM

LTP
Liturgy Training Publications

With gratitude to Gordon Lathrop

———————

Design by Jill Smith

Copyright © 1991 Archdiocese of Chicago. All rights reserved.
Liturgy Training Publications
1800 North Hermitage Avenue
Chicago IL 60622-1101
1-800-933-1800

ISBN 0-929650-28-X

Printed in the United States of America

CONTENTS

Introduction

I conclude this book on March 7, the day the church commemorates the martyrdom of Perpetua and Felicity. While in prison, Perpetua wrote an account of her visions, and she is remembered for her vivid images stepping on the head of the dragon, drinking the sweet milk of the shepherd. I follow after her, not striding into the arena, but writing of the hope that is in me, seeking for images to carry the praise.

During the early centuries of the church, apologists, theologians and bishops wrote and preached on the meaning of the eucharistic liturgy. This is what we mean, said Justin, Ambrose, Cyril and so many others, when we meet on Sunday, when we say these words, when we chant these songs. Our century has returned to this form of catechesis, as pastoral liturgists offer meditations about the Mass, so that the faithful may know more fully the mystery of the meal. We write in a modern search for meaning, but we learn much from the past. I follow after Ambrose, not concurring with much of his worldview, but echoing his metaphoric use of scriptural images to explicate the meanings of the liturgy.

On Perpetua's Day, with a thank-you to Ambrose, I welcome you to the liturgy.

Sunday

Perhaps it is a baby's cry, yelping for milk, that awakens us on Sunday morning. Perhaps it is a tipsy driver backing into garbage cans, or one's beloved moving about in bed, or an early fishing boat motoring across the lake, or a television commercial for children's cereal. Or perhaps it is the alarm clock, calling us with baroque music or yesterday's news to the barn or the sacristy or the kitchen. What comes first to consciousness? Dream images? Yesterday's quarrels? A list of chores? The morning psalm? And then we know: It is Sunday morning.

Wallace Stevens wrote a complicated poem about a woman's daydreams on Sunday morning. "Complacencies of the peignoir," begins the poem entitled "Sunday Morning." As you might suspect, the woman doesn't rush to get dressed and dash off to Mass. "We live in the chaos of the sun," she concludes after ruminations on nature, art, religion, Christ. She remains in her nightgown, preferring life and death as she knows it to the tomb in Palestine, for "divinity must live within herself." In "Church Going," another contemporary poet, Philip Larkin, does enter a church, but only as a curious tourist, "once I am sure there's nothing going on." He ponders the empty building.

. . . wondering too
When churches fall completely out of use
What we shall turn them into.

"Man's heart expands to tinker with his car, for this is Sunday morning," writes Louis MacNeice in another poem entitled "Sunday Morning." So it is that the poets of our century, while acknowledging the mythic power of Sunday morning, admit its emptiness for them.

But we, well, we are different. We pop out of bed and get ready for worship. As a small child reared in a pro-Protestant, anti-Catholic atmosphere, I heard that "Catholics *have* to go to church, but we *want* to go to church." Of that I know only that in my pious home we were absolutely required to want to go to church, thus enjoying the double whammy with which some religious traditions swat their children. So I wonder, rearing my daughters, how to pass down, in this secular age with its poems despairing of Christ, the significance of Sunday morning. I want them to hear not only the drones of agnostic authors, but also the metaphors of Christians throughout the ages singing the meaning of Sunday.

In about 150 CE, Justin, a layman, wrote a treatise to the Roman emperor defending the Christian faith. Of Christian worship he wrote, "On the day called Sun-day an assembly is held in one place." This is old stuff, Christians meeting on Sunday. Biblical scholars see in the Lucan and Johannine narratives of the post-resurrection appearances of Christ a pattern already made: It is on Sunday that Christians assemble around the risen Lord. On that first resurrection Sunday the disciples of Emmaus knew their Lord in the breaking of the bread. "On the first day of the week" Jesus appeared to the disciples behind locked doors, and "eight days later" Jesus confronted Thomas.

Luke 24:13

John 20:19
John 20:26

Americans on vacation visiting reconstructed Pilgrim villages hear about the late-Reformation tendency to turn Sunday into a Sabbath. Blue laws may keep liquor stores closed on Sunday, and in Lake Wobegon it is a crime to hang wash on the line on Sunday. But of course in its origin Sunday was not the Sabbath. For early Christians Saturday was the Sabbath, the Jewish day of rest, a phenomenal gift of Israel's God to the chosen people in a world marked by the unceasing struggle to survive. In contrast, Sunday was a workday, the regular secular day of life in the world, on which the faithful assembled, before the workday

Exodus 20:11–12

began or late Saturday evening when Sabbath was completed, to feast around the risen Christ.

The names of the days of the week evolved down to our time from ancient astrology, indicating to us belief in the power of the planets over human destiny. Each day of the week was assigned to a heavenly being, and the sun, assumed to be the planet closest and most powerful, was granted authority over the first day of the week. No more then than now, I believe, human-kind worships the sun's power: Whether with solar heating panels, crowded summer beaches, carefully positioned gardens, or endless sunset photographs, we attest to the bond of all earth's life to the sun. I lived once in an apartment high on a hill and with many windows opening to the east and west, and I came finally in midlife to know the sun, to mark its course on the horizon, to heed its schedule, to discover myself ill at ease after an overcast week. In midwinter we beg for the sun's return. Indeed, people's celebrations at the winter solstice are the back-drop for the church's designation of the shortest day of the year as the birthday of Christ. Although Christmas is not a "Sunday" feast, it has played a part in our archetypal bond to the sun. I am delighted that the secularizing attempt to position the week as beginning with Monday has not swept over us yet, and I ask you to join me in buying as calendars only the old-fashioned kind in which the week begins with the sun's day.

Justin offers a trinity of reasons to explain why Christians assemble on Sunday. On Sunday God began creation, calling light out of darkness; on Sunday Christ rose from the dead, bringing life out of the grave; on Sunday Christ taught the disci-ples, forming a faithful community out of a fragmented band. It was also on a Sunday, the "fiftieth day"—Pentecost—that the Spirit came. Some Christians called Sunday not the first day, as in creation, but the eighth day, as in the eschaton, the day signaling the beginning of a new age, a week as yet unnamed, old patterns broken, the future not yet here but miraculously already enjoyed. Sunday: the beginning of life, of creation, of light, of human reckoning, of social organization, of a new cycle of hope beyond human structure.

About 500 BCE, Malachi wrote of his hope that God would come to the temple rendering judgment on the people. "But for you who fear my name, the sun of righteousness will rise, with *Malachi 4:2* healing in its wings." Malachi stretches the sun image in the manner of a great poet: The sun will also rise on those in darkness, and the sun will bring not only natural light but the spiritual illumination of righteousness, and not only righteousness but healing, that powerful sun soaring with immense mythical wings. Literature teachers would scold Malachi for his mixed metaphors, suns and birds and health and justice all intermingled. Thus some modern translators tame the metaphor, substituting the sun's "rays" for the wings in the Hebrew text. I say let the crazy line stand, the sun's wings healing us with righteousness. We need such mingling of metaphors in our stuttering about God.

Malachi's line is a summary description of the Sunday liturgy. All these same images are mingled in Psalm 36, in which we see light by being in God's light, where under God's wings we *Psalm 36:7–9* feast in God's house and drink from the river of divine delight. I do not mean to say Malachi thought he was describing our liturgy: He was babbling out of his hope that God would come to save the people. But using the technique theologians call typology, the church uses Malachi's image to describe our experience of grace.

So on the day called Sun-day we assemble. We come for enlightenment, we come for healing of body and spirit, we come for righteousness before God and justice among the peoples. And how does this Sunday miracle arrive? On wings: astonishingly, in Christ's resurrection and the Spirit's descent. We use an inappropriate metaphor to suggest the bizarre phenomenon, that in this assembly we are flown by God into light and health and justice, for we are carried by the Spirit into the outstretched arms of Christ. The arms of Christ held to the cross are the wings of the Spirit, our transport into one another and finally into the very being of God.

All this ecstatic utterance, arms of Christ and wings of the Spirit: How does this describe our Sunday morning? For Christian worship is not in fact a levitation into cloudy heaven. We touch the wings of God in the arms of the ushers collecting our offering for the poor, in the hands of our neighbors giving us the greeting of peace, in the fingers of the minister laying bread in our palms, in the embraces of other worshipers on our way to the car. Sunday begins each week anew with the faithful pattern of receiving God's body in our lives by giving to the poor and by consoling a neighbor and by embracing another human being. The liturgy reminds us of the priorities of the baptized: Under God's light we live together righteously. It is not that we line up in rows like soldiers yelled at by the drill sergeant at a noonday review of the troops. It is that we huddle together, even when it is not pouring rain or beastly cold, and best of all at the midnight of Easter, to praise the light of Christ, of which the natural sun is only a meager metaphor. John's vision of the new Jerusalem foresees that in heaven there will be no sun at all. The city *Revelation 22:5* will be beyond the need of the sun, "for the glory of God is its light, and its lamp is the Lamb." (There's another mixed metaphor to think about some time!) So it is for Christians on Sunday morning.

O bright God,
O burning God,
O resplendent God,
accompany us, shrouded in darkness,
by the night of Calvary.
Transfigure our chaos,
illumine our tombs,
and fly us arm in arm into your life,
through Christ the living one.

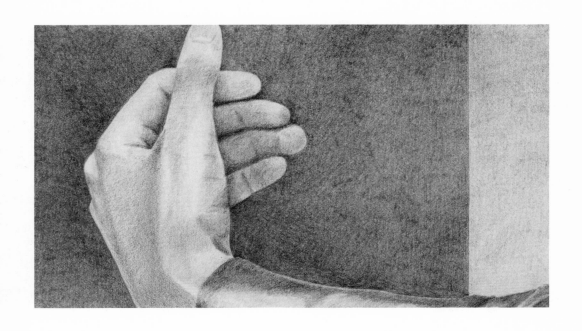

The Name

We begin the liturgy under the sign of the cross and with the words, "In the name of the Father, and of the Son, and of the Holy Spirit." At each liturgy we are, with the wailing infant or the enthusiastic catechumen, again at the baptismal beginning, under the cross and in the name. The phrase accompanying our sign of the cross could be more simply explanatory, like, "Today we stand again beside Mary and John on Calvary," or, with Paul, "We bear on our bodies the marks of Jesus," or echoing Constantine, "In this sign conquer." But instead we speak oblique words, a phrase not directly related to our gesture. Yet this many-layered phrase has come to be the church's way to speak with Mary, John, Paul, Constantine, and all history's throngs who stand at the foot of the cross.

In Ursula LeGuin's *A Wizard of Earthsea*, the young wizard comes to have power in the universe by learning the true names of things. Speaking the true names from the Old Speech, the wizard can control the weather, the animals, sickness, even the spirits of the dead; for everything must respond when addressed by its true name. To have the name is to know the thing's very being; and thus to have power, one speaks the name. The wizard's magical mastery with words would sound believable to those in preliterate times speaking Semitic languages. Before words were written down, becoming the staid and flat labels we now think they are, spoken names were thought to be an essential part of the thing, like the skeleton, or the soul. Adam knows each animal and thus can name it, and a change in human character is signified by a change in name, as Jacob becomes Israel and Saul becomes Paul.

Genesis 2:19–20

Genesis 32:28

Acts 13:9

We still see traces of the primitive power of "the name." There is your given name. In analysis, family therapists inquire into the stated or hidden reasons for the names that parents gave their children. Did your grandparent's name come to you as gift, obligation, regret? There is your surname. When my college's alumnae listing comes in the mail, I smile over the current confusion over married women's names: One never knows which of many options a couple will choose to signify their true names. (I have a friend who teased that new marriage rites should include the question, "By what name shall this couple be called?")

Of course it is in poetry that the magical power of words to indicate reality is most delightfully evident. My sixth-grade daughter recently studied "Jabberwocky," and there in the beamish boy galumphing back with his vorpal blade we hear the power of the word, although the word is not a real word at all. Even in our computer-screen times, some words have absolute creative power: Linguistic philosophers call "performance utterances" such mighty phrases as "I love you," "I forgive you," "I take you to be my husband."

Genesis 4:26
Genesis 12:7
The ancient idea of the power of "the name" permeates the Bible. In Genesis Adam's grandson and later Abraham begin "to call upon the name of YHWH." Remember when children addressed adults as Mr. or Miss, and when calling someone by her first name was an intentional sign of closeness? This was Israel's joy, being on a first-name basis with the God of the universe. The divine name was a sign of God's self-disclosure, a gift of God's grace, but like Mt. Sinai with its magnificent grandeur, *Exodus 19:12* one built a fence around it. Thus, the rabbis, like modern devout Jews, never pronounced the name, but spoke the title "LORD" instead. Hundreds of times in the Hebrew Scriptures "the name of the LORD" is evoked and praised. Solomon builds the temple *1 Kings 5:5* as a place to house the name of the LORD, and the thrilling contest between Elijah and Jezebel's prophets, in which bulls are

ritually sacrificed, tests which group has power over which name of divinity, Baal or YHWH.

1 Kings 18:20–40

The power of "the name" continues in the New Testament, as the disciples believe in, teach, baptize and are martyred "in the name of Jesus." Jesus is the one, we sing during the eucharistic prayer, "who comes in the name of the Lord," and we come trailing along in the name of Jesus. Peter and John say to the lame man, "In the name of Jesus Christ of Nazareth, rise and walk," and the man leaps up, dancing around the temple. As it says in an early Christian creed, Christ Jesus received "the name above every name." For Christians in calling Jesus "Lord" are giving the crucified man the first name of God.

Acts 3:6

Philippians 3:9–11

But stay with me. There is yet another amazing part of this divine name. In Exodus, God is disclosed to Moses out of the burning bush as the God of mercy and liberation, and when Moses asks for God's name, we hear the YHWH translated: I AM. God is the I AM, the one who is. An astonishingly modern name in this ancient story, anticipating the obsessive query of western philosophers and writers: Who am I anyway? God is. When Jesus says, "Before Abraham was, I am," they take up stones to throw at him, for he has assumed the divine name. When Jesus answers the high priest, "You say that I am," the court can convict him of blasphemy. To be fully, to be completely, is to be God. God is. I AM.

Exodus 3:14

John 8:58

Luke 22:70

One more step. In Jesus the church has come to know the God of the burning bush as Trinity. Surely exceeding nonsense has been taught and imagined about what this mystery signifies. One summer I saw on the wall of a German church which was important to the Reformers, next to a portrait of Luther, a picture of the Trinity, with God wearing a papal crown, Jesus on the cross below, and the dove flying about. Really, now! One appreciates anew the fence around the name. Rather, what is revealed in the Spirit of Jesus is that God's I AM is known in the relationships of love. Divine being is not about serene isolation, Zeus arbitrarily raining thunderbolts, the Thinker meditating on the world's woes. Rather, being—as God intended it—is mutual love, interdependent communion, one which is known only in three, and the three being open to the whole world. Two would be easier for us to imagine; a divine couple is typical religious mythology. But three? The divine dance of the three in love, and so being I AM, this is the Christian mystery to ponder.

In baptism we are reborn and given a new name. Christians, we call ourselves. We live both under our own name, with all its personal associations (are you a Fannie Mae? a Joy? an Ignatius? a Poopsy?) and under the name of Jesus, and so under the divine name itself. And when I am ashamed of who I am, and when my name is shoveled about, my comfort is not only that such is the lot of all children of humanity. Rather, my comfort rests in God's baptismal claim, the I AM, divine mercy, which gives me a family far beyond the wholesome or dreadful human family which is mine, a family of all those who in God are named with Christ's name, and finally, the family of God's loving self.

God's name is for us a womb. A womb, not a safe: God's name does not seal us off in some spiritual space capsule, suspended from any danger. No, the name of Jesus is like a womb, letting in both the calcium and the alcohol. They say now that the fetus can hear music played in the room, and so the baby is born predisposed to Bach or rock. So we who bear the name of Jesus hear the cries of the poor and the dying, the obnoxious aunt and the incoherent beggar. We who live in the power of the divine name are mightily weak in this world, one of the poor and the dying ourselves. We who in baptism take identity from God's I AM come *to be* only in interrelationships of love, needing one another to be at all.

The penitential rite which begins many western liturgies can be thought of as an enactment of the story of Cain. Cain, after killing his brother Abel in that primordial transgression within the human community, escapes, afraid for his life, guilty, running. And God puts a mark on Cain, that none would slay him. Perhaps this mark was on his forehead, a sign both of Cain's guilt and of God's mercy. Thus the penitential rite. For through baptism there is a merciful mark on our foreheads, the mark which will shine forth clearly only at the end of time in the dominion of God. There on our foreheads shall be God's name. We see that mark only by faith now, behind the wrinkles and makeup and dirt. The mark is there, on all the foreheads in our assembly, on all the foreheads of baptized Christians throughout the world, at every baptism and every eucharist we celebrate. The mark of Cain becomes the name of God, the primitive power of God's name binding us.

Genesis 4:2–15

Revelation 22:4

O sacred Mystery,
O Being infinite,
O One who loves and is loved and is love,
we dance inside your name,
we kiss its consonants in one another.
Help us to bear your name in Jesus,
and at our end nail up your name on our cross,
through Christ our Lord.

Living Water

It is Sunday and we have assembled in the name of Christ. Many of us are now ready to do the customary ritual: to begin our communal thanksgiving with a confession of sins. Not that Christians always opened their assembly with confession and absolution: quite the contrary. In fact, during the church's early decades theologians fervently debated whether baptized people were any longer capable of sin. There came to be agreement that there were three most grievous sins—apostasy, murder and adultery—which even the most enthusiastic believer could observe in the community, and rituals of public penance were developed to deal with these public sinners. Long years of intro-spection lengthened the list of postbaptismal sins until Augustine schooled the Western world into selves wholly reflec-tive of inevitable sin. Yet even after Augustine the Sunday assembly did not open with confession.

It was actually not until the eleventh century, when cleri-calism in the West became a high art and the priest's ritual purity a neo-Levitical obsession, that the priest opened the lit-urgy with a private prayer, begging that he be worthy to celebrate the Mass. The Reformation principle of reevaluating clerical position took this stance away from the priest and made of it a general confession for all the faithful. The medieval piety was not transformed, but transferred from the priest to the assembly. Contemporary Roman Catholics have followed this Reformation pattern, generalizing the priest's Confiteor into a confessional Kyrie. Confession is now cast in stone, the rock of the whole church a figure kneeling, bowed, weekly begging for-giveness and pleading unworthiness before God. In the Lutheranism of my childhood, I confessed at each communion service "all my sins and iniquities with which I have ever offended Thee," last week's absolution apparently not having made a dent in the prisonhouse of my incessant guilt.

Liturgical rituals and texts express certain biblical and cultural truths, but at the expense of other truths. And so recent liturgical reforms in all the churches have hoped to open up this narrow crawl space leading to the Sunday assembly. Protestants have stressed that the confession is not obligatory and is more appropriate for some seasons than for others. The Roman Catholic sacramentary provides Option A, the rite in which water is sprinkled over the people amid prayers recalling baptism and pleading for God's life for the whole created order. But this reform lags. For though we are too familiar with the self-image of kneeling, we are distant from the sound of flowing water, so stiff in the knee joints that we cannot stand tall as God's water rains upon us. We need to be reborn by the well of living water.

In ancient times, in a dry land, the well was the town's meeting place, a locus for the community's exchanges, the place that death was traded for life. Jacob meets Rachel at the well and falls in love at first sight. Moses protects Zipporah from some ruffians at a well and later marries her. Hagar is saved from death when God miraculously causes a well to appear. When the people of Israel are groaning from thirst, Moses strikes a rock, from which flows living water. If wells full of water are reservoirs of life, then empty wells are prisons, prospective tombs, as Joseph, pitched into an empty well by his jealous brothers, and Jeremiah, lowered into a dry cistern by the king's men, unhappily discover. In some of the stories, the well is a sign of the power of human love. Abraham's servant Eliezer is sent to find a wife for Isaac. He sits at the well of Nabor; the shepherd Rebekah comes with water jars; he asks for a drink, and she gives it. When the conversation is concluded, she rushes home

Genesis 29:1–20

Exodus 2:15–21

Genesis 21:9–21

Numbers 20:2–13

Genesis 37:12–24

Jeremiah 35:1–6

Genesis 24

to tell her family that she has found her life at the well. Match-maker Eliezer arranges the engagement: Rebekah is to marry Isaac and produce sons. What more of life could this young shepherd desire?

Christians know a similar story: Jesus, weary with travel, sits down at Jacob's well in Samaria, and after asking a woman for water to drink, engages with her in a theological discussion concerning the hopes of the chosen people. The woman, surprised that a Judean man is talking to a woman—and a Samaritan woman at that—gives him water from the cistern. But she would be glad of living water, flowing water, a fountain of life, liberating her from the daily arduous task of lugging home heavy jars of well-water. When the conversation concludes, she rushes home to tell her neighbors that she has found her life at the well. Come to the waters, she calls out in the streets of her town.

John 4:1–42

Isaiah 55:1

The Samaritan woman claimed to have found her living water. Was she singing, along with the lover in the Song of Songs, that her beloved was "a garden fountain, a well of living water, and flowing streams from Lebanon"? Clearly she meant other than her matriarchs Rebekah and Rachel, who rejoiced to have found their life's love at the well. The Samaritan woman had tried and tried to find a life's love, but now is looking for more. The water in John 4, this fountain of life, is more than a backdrop for courtship or a sign of human connection; and like all archetypal religious symbols, the water becomes even more for us than it was for the Samaritan woman.

Song of Songs 4:15

The Hebrew tradition used the image of the fountain of life to describe the word of God. The Torah is living water, the pious Jew would say. The fourth evangelist, knowing well the history of Hebrew metaphors, plays with this: Do you wish to drink up divine joys? Have you come looking in the words of Moses for

Sirach 24:21

the life of God? Here I am, says Jesus; I am the Word of God speaking the word of God while sitting at the well of the patriarch Jacob. Drink up my words and live. Come to these waters to quench your deepest thirst.

Christians came to apply the language of "living water" to baptism. The baptistry found in the excavations at Dura Europos depicts over the great basin the woman sitting at the well. It is the baptismal waters that satisfy the thirsty woman and that revive the faithful in that final and glorious city of God. Baptism is the birthwaters of Nicodemus, the drowning of the old Adam, the cleansing which Hebrew ritual required, the floodwaters signifying Christ's resurrection. Like water in the womb, God's water is our matrix, washing all of us together, protecting us from harm, both surrounding us and filling us with life.

Revelation 21:6

John 3:5

1 Peter 3:21

Suddenly I recall my only experience with scarcity of water. In the Connecticut of my youth, the reservoirs were not sufficient for the communities' needs. August meant prohibitions against watering gardens, prayers for rain in all the churches, and bad-tasting drinking water. Then my family would drive outside of town to a rocky promontory in the woods and fill a great canning kettle with spring water that flowed, it seemed to me, right out of a rock. The black kettle was kept in the dark back entry, and we ladled out this water only for drinking, this crisp, clean, living water. That our family had water from the rock was a sign to me that soon the rains would come.

The Jews in the first century practiced a ritual that sounds something like such sympathetic magic. At the Feast of Tabernacles, water by the pitcherful was carried up to the temple mound and poured down its steps, that the people would remember the water from the rock and that God would remember to send the autumn rains. This was a ritual of living water, powerful for a people who knew drought. John's gospel records that "on the last day of the feast, the great day," Jesus called the thirsty to him. From his heart would pour living water, from his heart would flow the Spirit. John's gospel knows that not only John and Mary stand at the foot of the cross. In fact we are among the millions there, sharing the Spirit, becoming family to each other, who are revived by the water flowing from his side.

John 7:37–39

John 19:26, 27, 34

Orthodox Jewish women have the custom of ritual bathing in a women's bathhouse after their monthly period. The Jewish mystics say that all water flows from the Garden of Eden and all washings are reimmersion into God's creative waters. The women's bathings begin again the cycle of life. And we too hear the call: Come all who are thirsty, all who are dry; come, you birthing, and come, you dying. Here is living water. Stand tall together, and be sprinkled or doused or soaked by the living water. Paradise is here, and these the waters flowing by the tree of life.

O God,
midwife and washerwoman and mountain spring,
over and over we must be born,
over and over we must be washed,
day after day we thirst.
The deer drink from your streams,
the fish live in your sea.
Deliver us, covered with your blood and water,
cleansed and full of grace,
at this our River Jordan.

Christ

My name I know, but what is my title? Dr., Ms., Mrs.? Which captures more of the truth—writer, liturgist, teacher, mother, wife? We wear titles like clothing, sometimes like coronation robes, sometimes like ill-fitting hand-me-downs. With our fascination for complex identities, we know that titles are incomplete, that they speak only part of the truth, that they mask their opposite. Although the appropriate title may gain us an invitation to the White House, the next eager news reporter may uncover how ineptly we fit into that title. Yet society needs such titles; and when a lecturer is paid $500 for a speech, the audience wants to know who and what this lecturer is.

My neighbor fares no better than I. I give you a title, I stick you in a jar with a neat label, and you squirm around, wanting a differently shaped container. I call you mom, or Father, or house-cleaner, or police officer, and I think I've got you down, knowing who and what you are. And you stand before me, begging to be released from the jar. Psychologists call "projection" our inclination to project onto our neighbor an image of the other which we have concocted in our head: When we hear the title bishop or doctor or vagrant, our little computer-brains flash on our mental screen a picture of such a person, and we do not see our neighbor without first looking through our meager mental image. No wonder we expend so much energy squirming, with people all day long projecting their needs onto us until their images of us weigh us down, leaden mantles on our souls.

We label God. One could construct a history of religions by organizing the progression of humankind's labels for God. There was Tree Spirit, Earth Mother, Thunderbolt, Prime Mover. The nomads seek a Rock, the city-dwellers a King, the diseased a Savior. Much of religion is this: projecting out into the sky or onto certain holy folk our great need for a benevolent universe.

In coming to know its need, humanity settles on its contemporary label for God, beseeching that titled divinity to order chaos or to forgive sins or to heal sickness or to end injustice. God must smile at our meager divine titles, for God's love and power are quite before and beyond the labels we choose, just as our need is exceedingly more than our current jargon can suggest.

One whom Christians struggle to label is Jesus of Nazareth.

Mark 8:27

"Who do people say that I am?" asks Jesus of his disciples then and now. Peter's sermons, Paul's letters, the evangelists' narratives, the ecumenical councils, our own parish liturgy committee: We all seek the way to title this Jesus who was crucified. "Joshua" was his Hebrew name, this Jewish man, and his given name evokes the hopes for the triumphant conqueror who will at last lead the people across the Jordan into the land of

Joshua 3:7–17
Deuteronomy 34:4–6

promise. For the people's great leader Moses finally failed: He died before bringing the people into the new land. Now we place our hopes in Joshua, Joshua of Nazareth.

The primary title the church grants Jesus of Nazareth is Christ. "Christ" is our label, shorthand to encapsulate our faith in this Joshua, a code name for an entire file drawer (see John's

John 1:29–51

account of Jesus' baptism!) of resplendent titles. "Christ, have mercy," we plead as the liturgy begins. The title has a long religious history, forgotten by our careless catechesis, until children think that Christ is Jesus' family name. "Christ" is Greek— interesting that we have only transliterated the Greek letters, we have not translated the title into American English—for the Hebrew title "the anointed one." In the ancient Semitic culture Aaron and his priests were anointed, sacred oil poured on their heads as a sign that in them the community perceived the Spirit of God. The shepherd boy David was anointed to be king one

Leviticus 8:10–13
1 Samuel 16:12–13

day, and increasingly in the Hebrew poetry of longing, "the

anointed one" was the title given to the one who will come in the name of the LORD to reign in peace and justice with the benevolent might of God. This glorious title is the one we give to Jesus: "You are the Christ," we say with Peter.

Mark 8:29

To be anointed in the Davidic line is to be king. "The King of the Jews" was Jesus' identification on the cross. The church has used the title of king for the one we call Christ, and there is a long history of liturgical art which depicts Christ as king. There were, during the fourteenth and fifteenth centuries, picture books drawn to encourage the devout in their meditation: These *Biblia Pauperum* were designed to proclaim the meaning of Christ by flanking a story from the life of Jesus with several stories from the Hebrew Scriptures which utilized the same images. So on the page depicting the visit of the magi to the infant Jesus there are also pictures of commander Abner acclaiming David king and of the Queen of Sheba offering treasures to King Solomon. Popular imagination drew the magi as kings honoring the King, and we sing "We Three Kings" because the early preachers saw in Isaiah 60 and Psalm 72 pictures of foreign monarchs coming to praise the anointed one. The old Hebrew stories gave Christians a way to picture Jesus. In the same way, from the ancient phrase "the anointed one" comes Jesus' title.

Mark 15:26

2 Kings 3:6–21

Chronicles 10:1–12

Yet Jesus squirms under this title, for it expresses only part of the truth. Jesus was not literally anointed a king. Early in the New Testament period "anoint" is already used as a metaphor. Peter preaches that "God anointed Jesus of Nazareth with the Holy Spirit and with power." Perhaps this sermon means to recall Jesus' baptism. The historic liturgy also calls baptism an anointing, and whether or not chrism is actually used at a baptism, all Christians can speak of having been anointed at baptism with the Spirit of Jesus.

Acts 10:38

Mark 14:3–9

The only actual anointing Jesus had was performed by the woman with the alabaster jar of very costly ointment. Perhaps we could think of the woman's alabaster jar of costly ointment as the vehicle of God's anointing of Jesus. As Jesus himself said, "Wherever the gospel is preached in the whole world, what she has done will be told in memory of her." Already in the gospel narrative Jesus does not sit well under the title "the anointed one," just as the crown and robe he wore for his passion alter our image of royal raiment.

What do you suppose "Christ" means to North American Christians? It is easier to make up a comic multiple-choice response than to answer the question. (I recall the mock theology exam published by Daniel Berrigan years ago in *Katallagete* in which one question was "Has the church always taught anything? Explain and be specific.") Christ is the anointed one who was only oddly, metaphorically, anointed, the one who comes in the name of the LORD to die. We borrow an ancient Hebrew metaphor as the title for the one who answers all human woe: Christ. We stand with centuries of the children of humanity and speak a title in an archaic tongue: Christ. We Christians take on this title as our own self-identification. The history of the title is easier to articulate than its future: What do you and I mean by our faith in "Christ"?

I wish I could hear from you all, collect all the hopes for fulfillment hiding in this title for Jesus, bring them all together like alms in a basket, and carefully lay them at the foot of the altar, that God would see and heed. "Remember the Messiah," cry our Jewish cousins to God, and we too in the eucharistic prayer beseech God to remember the one anointed to bring a time of peace and a space for praise. How I would say it is this:

God has promised to save the world. Far before whatever categories we dream up, God's word has already formed in the communion of the faithful the hope of a new earth: not a second Eden, but a heavenly earthly city, human life at its fullest, twelve gates to accommodate the mobs, jewels enough to waste on building facades, streets of pure gold. We call this hope by many names: heaven, the second coming, forgiveness, deification, the millennium, the resurrection, the dominion and reign and rule and kingdom of Christ. We who act patronizing about twentieth-century monarchs use the ancient human language as our alabaster jar, offering to God our hope that in the anointed one will come our peace and our justice and our joy.

Yet fortunately the prayer itself pleads beyond our imaginings. We do not say "Christ, come to reign," or "Christ, let me sit at your right hand in your dominion." With one voice we say "Christ, have mercy." And so the Kyrie itself is a plea beyond our titles for God, an acknowledgment of the God who is and was and will be far beyond our meager projections. It is a stroke of divine humor that God's mercy comes to us in the oddly anointed Joshua of Nazareth. May the incongruity of God's way of anointing bend our projections of what religion is all about that we may see, sneaking into our banquet hall, the beggar at our feet.

Christ, have mercy.
The world has run out of sacred oil,
and we bring only neediness in our alabaster jar.
Be pleased to receive such anointing:
Christ, have mercy.

Glory

Glory: the shimmering gold stones of the floor-to-ceiling mosaics in the holy places of Ravenna. Glory: the flowered islands of the Lady and Unicorn tapestries encircling you in the round room in the Paris museum. Glory: Elizabeth II being anointed by the Archbishop of Canterbury in that little tent in Westminster Abbey, my earliest international memory. Glory: the sunset new each evening over the sky, which glory was, I suppose, there all the years I didn't think to watch it.

When liturgists use the word "glory," it is often as the adjective "glorious," as in the phrase "Oh, it was a glorious liturgy!" Of course, liturgy planning and critique are never dull since all of us on the committee have mutually exclusive opinions about what constitutes glorious liturgy. What do you hear as glorious: state trumpets, Bach motets, Latin chant, Berthier canons, revival songs, conga drums, Victorian hymnody? Newly formed liturgy committees might well benefit from a roundtable discussion entitled: "What is glorious liturgy?" The games committees play in planning liturgies together might be less frustrating were we to know everyone's strong suit at the outset.

To some, glorious liturgy is about splendor, even pomp; to others, glory is the dark quiet of a holy womb. St. Mary Major in Rome, or the church at Taizé? Once in touring Newport, Rhode Island, I visited on one day both the Breakers, the most opulent seaside estate of the robber-baron era, and the Quakers, the nineteenth-century meeting house of the plain people. Which edifice was more glorious?

In trying to determine what is and what is not glorious, liturgy committees continue in the present day the age-old religious quest for the glory of God. From earthly darkness we search for divine glory; from human misery we plead for that glory; aware of the humbling fact of death we aspire for the glory of God. Religions bow down before theophanies, build towers to reach God and temples to honor God, authorize priestly sorts to represent God's glory. Christianity shares with many other religions this predilection to capture God's glory, this gilding of churches, these gems on the holy things. Karl Marx concluded that the primary object of religion was to allow suffering human beings to glimpse a glory which could never be their own.

The Hebrew Scriptures record the ancient Jewish search for the glory of God. In the wilderness wanderings the glory of God *Exodus 16:10* resided in the cloud, and this mighty cloud in hovering around *Exodus 14:19–20* the people protected them from danger. The cloud of the glory of God separated Israel from the Pharaoh's army so that the east wind could blow the sea apart and make a dry passage to safety. *Exodus 33:9–11* Later this cloud covered and filled the holy tent, and as the tent became the locus of religious devotion, it is as if the glory of God transferred itself from the cloud directly to the tent itself. The tent is then only a step toward the temple, and at Solomon's dedication of the temple the cloud of the glory of *Kings 8:10–11* God filled the gilded edifice. And even though Solomon acknowledged that the temple cannot by any means contain God, the building became so identified with the glory of God *Lamentations 2:2–7* that when the temple was destroyed, the people were devastated. Sometimes the signs of the glory of God have worked too well!

The God of the Hebrew Scriptures, in a manner surprising among ancient religions, is benevolent to the people and glorious in deed. Quite apart from clouds of presence, the holy tent and the splendid building, this God is known through glorious narratives. God did these mighty deeds: Thus we tell the stories, sing the psalms, record the visions. That God sent Moses to free the slaves has more to do with our God than that a lonely shepherd saw a bush burning. Israel did not sculpt glorious representations of divinity, but rather recited the sagas of the glorious deeds of the LORD. Not lengthy descriptions of the divine nimbus, but Deborah's song and Hannah's song of the mighty acts of God: This is the way of the Hebrew Scriptures.

Psalm 136

Judges 5
1 Samuel 2:1–10

We Christians receive this tradition of the glory of God in cloud and deed. We know that the disciples, looking quizzically at Jesus, saw in their mind's eye the venerable vision of a Mighty One coming in the clouds in great power and glory, magnificently rescuing the people. And as we are wondering what the glory of Mount Sinai and the glory of the Coming One have to do with Jesus, we read John's gospel and learn again how prehistoric religious quests and the tradition of Israel give us words that burst their meanings in Christ. "We beheld his glory," says John's prologue. In Jesus is the glory of the word of God. And although the story of Cana's miracle suggests that Jesus' glory is seen in mighty deeds, Jesus' prayer in John 17 opens the word more deeply. What emerges is, strangely, a glory manifested in his death. Glorify me, prays Jesus. It would seem that in making decisions about glorious liturgy, our committees would have to remember a throne which is a cross. (Where did a bishop's "throne" come from then?)

Mark 9:1

John 1:14

John 17:5

But, you might ask, what is all this talk about the glory *of* God, when the classic hymn of praise begins "Glory *to* God"?

As the Hebrew prophets proclaimed, our God needs no offerings, does not eat our proffered food, does not require our liturgy. We can give no "glory to God." All we can do is to ascribe to God what God already is. As the seventeenth-century Westminster Catechism had it, "What is the chief end of man? Man's chief end is to glorify God and to enjoy him forever." We are to know the glory of God and to proclaim it to God and to one another.

It is as if our worship were a time of intentional mirroring of God. Corporate worship is the communal ritual of trying out our identity, renewing it, strengthening it, by together mirroring the glory of God. In worship we declare the image of God, that we might better know it in ourselves. We recite and enact what "glory" means in this assembly and with these religious words. On Sunday we mirror to God the very glory of God, and thus on Monday we are able to better reflect that glory. One classic way to understand the Fall is to acknowledge that we are unwilling to let God be God and humankind be humankind. In *Bedazzled*, the comedy about the Mephistopheles legend, Lucifer wearies of praising and glorifying God and says, "Hey, I'm getting a bit bored with this. Can't we switch places?" But in worship we take our created place, mirroring back, rather than absconding with, the glory of God. In the mirroring of God we know again our own self to have been created in the divine image. We need not swipe what has already been graciously given.

Genesis 1:27

Historians of liturgy teach us that the Gloria was a relatively late addition to the liturgy, and some current books of worship suggest options for the ancient "Glory to God." But in this I am conservative: I am caught by the tension between the "Lord, have mercy" and the "Glory to God." I hope to understand the still small voice of the breaking of bread as the explication of the organ and choir and assembly bellowing out "Glory!"

My favorite biblical story about the glory of God is in Exodus 33. Moses asks what we liturgists ask, what religions seek: "Show me your glory." God's answer? God will indeed show divine glory to Moses: "I will make all my goodness pass before you." Yet it is not splendiferous brilliance, blinding light, lightning explosions, that Moses will view, but God's goodness,

Exodus 33:17–23

32

graciousness and mercy. But even when God is seen in goodness, a human being cannot look on this divine glory and live. The sight is too much for us; we would burst apart. So God hides Moses in the cleft of the rock. And the rock was Christ, we say, for we too hide in Christ to behold God's glory. Hiding there in Christ we, along with Moses, see only God's backside, and that is enough for us now. For there on God's backside are the wounds of Jesus, made by the scourging of the Roman soldiers. Carried on God's backside are the water jars of Rebekah, pouring out water for Abraham's thirsty servant. Laden on God's backside are all those lost sheep that the shepherd has rescued from paths so foolishly taken.

1 Corinthians 10:4

John 19:1

Genesis 24:15–20

Luke 15:3–7

Finally, it has been promised us, in the end time it will not be God's backside that we see. "We shall see God's face," it says in Revelation. Perhaps then we will know the glory of the cloud, the temple, and the cross as fully as we are known.

Revelation 22:4

O God,
we hope to praise your glorious face
but instead magnify your wounded backside.
May we mirror your glory,
beholding you and ourselves
through Christ, the oddly shining one.

Word

Words are getting cheaper every day. Toddlers have plastic toys that croak out speech. Students with meager vocabulary and poor spelling merely insert editing diskettes into their computers, and lo! they receive the better grades that their snazzy programs deserve. Potboiler novels are produced at a pace never before possible, and television reporters on election night jabber successfully for hours and hours, saying absolutely nothing to millions of listeners. When I expressed moral outrage at the lyrics of a rock song, I ought not to have been surprised by my daughter's response: "But Mom, the words don't matter."

But long ago it was different. Think back before words multiplied out from laser printers like the brooms of the sorcerer's apprentice. Think back before the monk who, when illuminating Psalm 1 in the *St. Omer Psaltery,* adorned the B for "Blessed" with an entire tree of Jesse, kings and prophets and finally Mary bearing the letters of the ancient psalm forward to the Christian who was reading the book. Think back before words were drawn on animal skins or etched into clay. Back then, the spoken word was all that held human society together.

The spoken word was the symbol of human intelligence and the sign of human commitment. The Genesis story indicates human precedence in creation by saying that Adam names all the animals. Knowing their full nature, Adam encapsulates their being in a single word. When the matriarch Rebekah helps her favorite son Jacob impersonate his elder brother Esau in order to claim the patriarchal blessing, the old man Isaac cannot revoke the blessing that he has spoken over Jacob. The words are already working their power. Isaac can pronounce only lesser words, a meager blessing, over the distraught Esau. To give one's word is to give one's self. So today, what actually marries two people is not the gowns and the reception, the flowers and the

Genesis 2:19

Genesis 27:1–40

license, surely not the phrase "I pronounce you husband and wife," but the couple's simple words of promise spoken in the presence of others.

The ancient notion that people are known by their words became important in the Israelite description of God. For the most part rejecting the sexual imagery that was common in Canaan, the Jewish tradition saw not in God's sexual organs, but rather in God's spoken word the divine power of creation and *Psalm 33:6* salvation. The psalms say that God's word created the universe. *Genesis 1* "Let there be," and there was. When God speaks, the faithful respond. God calls Abraham, Moses, Samuel, and Isaiah, and hearing the word of God they say, "Here I am."

The word of God fills the prophet with divine power; it overflows to others, and the prophet speaks out that word. When the king Josiah despairs that the people have not been obeying the word of God, his priests seek out the prophet *2 Kings 22:14–20* Huldah. She proclaims to them the word of the LORD, a promise of peace and restitution to all who return to God. The prophet *Ezekiel 3:3* Ezekiel receives the word of God as a written scroll and eats it. In his mouth it is sweet as honey, and this ingested word Ezekiel proclaims. To preach the word of God is to get your mouth around God and proclaim God to others.

Luke narrates several stories that bring the ancient Israelite prophets' words into the present assembly. Jesus in the synagogue in Nazareth reads the promises of salvation from the prophet Isaiah and proclaims, "Today this scripture has been fulfilled in *Luke 4:16–21* your hearing." The word of God is fulfilled in the ministry of Jesus. But Luke's histories further show that even after the resurrection, the word of God continues on earth, creating and saving the world. The apostle Philip, not himself an Israelite but rather a Greek, instructs the Ethiopian eunuch in the meaning of the words of Isaiah 53. In explaining the song in Isaiah, Philip *Acts 8:26–39* preaches the good news of Jesus, and the eunuch's response to hearing the word of God is to ask for baptism.

These Lucan narratives would be especially surprising for devout hearers of God's ancient word. In the first story, the controversial Jesus is in the synagogue reading to other devout Jews from the Hebrew Scriptures. But in the second story, the preacher is not a Jew, but a Greek. Neither is the hearer a Jew; he is an Ethiopian. Furthermore, as a eunuch he is castrated, a second characteristic that according to the Torah would surely prohibit him from entering the assembly of the faithful. But Luke knows another prophetic passage in Isaiah, chapter 56. The *Isaiah 56:3–6* divine word promises that one day even the foreign eunuch will enter the house of God for prayer and praise.

Here then is one meaning of the phrase "This is the Word of the Lord." We are the foreigner, the eunuch. We are the powerless outsiders who have gathered around some readings from the Hebrew Scriptures, ancient tales and poems that speak of a benevolent universe and a merciful divinity. We hunger for the sweetness of Ezekiel's scroll. And although some assemblies expect a historical and critical introduction to the ancient words, it is not the origin of the passage or the century of transcription that matters. Rather, the assembly hears the word of God, and receives in that word the truth of Jesus Christ and comes to the font.

But there is more; in God there is always more. Several decades after Luke wrote that in Jesus is the word of God, the Johannine community sang a stronger song. Not only is Jesus *John 1:1–14* preaching the word of God, Jesus is the Word. That Word of God which created the world and shines in its darkness, that divine power for life, is Jesus Christ. When Christ speaks, it is

God who speaks. To know the Messiah is to know God. To listen to Jesus is to hear the word of God.

This language of John's prologue seized Martin Luther's imagination: The Word is Christ, Christ is the Word. In his famous hymn "A mighty fortress," a battle ensues in which the devil and all evil forces fight against the believers. Evil is conquered by "a word," by which Luther means Christ. The artists who crafted the *Bible Moralisee,* the thirteenth-century picture-Bible in which Old Testament stories were matched with New Testament narratives or contemporary church events, also knew of Christ as the Word. Next to the picture of Pharoah's daughter *Exodus 1:5–6* finding Moses in the basket was a picture of church folk discovering the infant Jesus lying in an open Bible. A depiction of the *Numbers 11:31–32* children of Israel consuming the quail in the wilderness is parallel to a picture of Christians hearing the word preached by the great Lady Church.

The readings for the Seventeenth Sunday in Ordinary Time of Year A present us with such a word. The first reading is *1 Kings 3:5–12* the narrative of King Solomon's dream, in which the young monarch is asked his fondest desire. Solomon prays for wisdom, and the word of the LORD praises his judgment. We follow this story by praying together an excerpt from Psalm 119. This long Wisdom psalm is constructed as a clever acrostic on the letters of the Hebrew alphabet and has in nearly every one of its 176 lines a synonym for the law of God. With the psalmist we praise God's word as a delight, a comfort, better than jewels, finer than gold, brighter than light. In praying the psalm we take the place of Solomon, choosing to honor the word of God.

But there is more, for it is as Christians that we read these *Matthew 13:44–52* ancient texts. The gospel reading contains two of Jesus' parables about "the kingdom of heaven," Matthew's way to talk about the power of God. Like the merchant who sells all for the pearl of great price, like the dragnet that hauls up everything in the sea: "Have you understood this?" Jesus asks. They, like we, too hastily say, "Yes, sure we do." But then comes another image of the word of God. Jesus suddenly talks about a scribe, that is, one who copies out and studies the word of God. We might think of the scribe who composed Psalm 119, of those who transcribed the Solomon story over the centuries, of Paul writing to the Romans, of Matthew himself, of all of us who delight in the word of God. The scribe, Jesus says, brings out of the household treasure both the new and the old: The old is the story of Solomon and the psalmist's praise of the word of God; the new is Jesus in our midst telling surprising stories, Jesus in our midst being the word of God.

Romans 8:28–30

The word is our treasure, our pearl of unsurpassed value. But a Martian visiting our liturgies would never guess it, with several mumbled sentences or a screeching microphone, with the first reading lost in the shuffle into pews and the rustling of pamphlets, and would be surprised when in a moment the people acclaim these words as the word of God. Can we identify those who are able to read with clarity and power? Can we be done with demeaning service folders? Can we sit up alert and attentive, eager to hear every word of the word? Can we teach this word to our children, telling them the stories of faith when we are sitting in our house and when we are walking by the way, when we lie down and when we rise?

Deuteronomy 11:18–19

We oddly accord honor to a collection of ancient words, little grains of sand stuck inside the shells of earlier days and other lands. For throughout the decades and centuries, some of those irritating stories and poems were found to be the pearls of Lady Wisdom, the divine word of power, the very presence of God.

We don the word, our pride and delight. We find ways to value the word, and discover in the attempt that we can give the word no value that it does not already have. We can only, like Solomon, be wise enough to recognize the power of the Spirit of God carried through the words to our expectant ears.

We know only human speech,
O divine Word.
To humor us, your little talkers,
squeeze your merciful might
into our small language,
that through the Spirit of that Word,
we may hear and live.

Gospel

In my fourth-grade Bible history textbook was an illustration of how the scriptures were written. The small but detailed drawing showed an old, heavily robed man writing intently with a quill pen on a large scroll, his white beard flowing down to the table top. The working of his pen was illuminated by a narrow but intense beam of light emanating from a haloed white dove perched near the rafters of his room. The Holy Spirit's brilliance guided the man's pen into sacred truth.

Theology courses in college suggested that the dove's beam was rather more diffuse. Storytellers—were they first mothers and fathers?—passed down stories over the centuries, sometimes altering tales borrowed from even more ancient peoples. Unknown scribes wrote narratives and poems, and unknown editors collated them into a vast array of books. Some of these works came to be revered as the people's central stories of faith and identity and thus were selected for public reading in their weekly and annual assemblies. For example, the creation story of Genesis 1 took precedence over the one recorded in the book of Jubilees, in which an extremely complicated sacred calendar with Wednesday as the week's primary day is the main obsession in the mind of God.

The Hebrew canon—that list of books deemed appropriate for reading in the religious assembly—was taking shape. Sometime before the birth of Christ, Jews translated their scriptures into Greek. One such translation is named the Septuagint (from the legend that at the request of the king of Egypt, 72 elders in 72 separate rooms each translated the Hebrew into identical Greek). Much like the picture in my textbook, this legend tells less of the method by which we got the scriptures than of the faith that God had a hand in their formation.

When Christians met weekly, as they had done in synagogue assemblies, they read from the Hebrew Scriptures the
gracious works of God. A full generation after Jesus' death,
Christians began to hear also pastoral letters from Paul. Two
generations after Jesus' death, compilations of the sayings and
stories of Jesus were introduced into the assemblies. How rapidly
these "New Testament" books circulated, we do not know. But it
was most likely four generations after the life of Christ before
our gospel of John, absolutely essential to later orthodox Christianity, circulated in the church. Thus the good news of the
resurrection was proclaimed by hearts and mouths for decades
before it was read from books.

1 Thessalonians 1:5   Paul's letters speak already about "the gospel," the Greek
word *evangelion* referring to the good news of God's salvation in
Christ. Mark's narrative, which most scholars agree is the first
completed of our four, uses the word gospel in its opening verse,
and the word comes to mean both the good news and the books
which narrate the good news. Our English word "gospel," from
the Anglo-Saxon "good-spell," was an exact translation of the
apostles' and evangelists' idea of "good tidings." Eventually from
the various narratives of Christ written in the first centuries, the
church selected four—our Matthew, Mark, Luke and John—as
canonical, appropriate for reading in the assembly. Some of the
others are easily available now in libraries and bookstores—the
gospels of Peter, of Thomas, of Mary, of Philip. Others may have
existed which are now lost. The assortment indicates how varied
were the images of Jesus and the meanings of his life for the
early Christian community.

Our contemporary lectionary has made the church more
aware than it was in the past that there are four gospel narratives. Most Christians, lay and clergy, for much of the church's

life knew the story of Jesus from harmonized retellings. But we are newly conscious of Matthew's focus on Jesus as the fulfillment of Old Testament promises, Mark's presentation of a hidden Messiah, Luke's emphasis on Jesus as the Savior of the whole world, and John's poetic stories and discourses on the relationship of Jesus to God. Homilists are trained to detect the specific slant of each gospel. We feel it clearest in Holy Week, when in successive years Passion Sunday gives us Matthew's promised king, Mark's hidden Christ, or Luke's redeeming savior, with Good Friday always offering us John's triumphant Son of God. The lectionary arranges Matthew, Mark and Luke around the great gospel of John, which as the richest jewel is worn annually on Christmas, Good Friday, the Easter Sundays and Pentecost, and is laid out for the catechumens to inspect during the season of Lent.

But just as the gospels themselves are concerned not with modern biographical or psychological questions about Jesus but with the meaning of Christ for the community, so the Christian assembly is concerned not with speculations about who the gospel writers were. Surely the historical-critical study of the Bible has helped us understand the message of Christ, for we know better the matrix out of which the words were written. But we balance attention to the evangelists as men limited by their experience with the church's faith that the Bible was inspired by God. The church, like my schoolbook illustration, honors the evangelist as a mouthpiece of God's benediction, a recorder of God's gracious power in the world.

The committees working on lectionary revision feel this tension acutely. We cannot read the full Bible during the liturgy; there must be selection, rejection, priority, editing. Which sections shall we select? Why? How much of the biblical worldview is essential to proclaim as indicative of the mind of God? I find it a mercy that none of the churches using a three-year lectionary include the passage from 1 Timothy about a woman being saved through childbearing, but the churches disagree about whether to include other passages about the created precedence of men over women. What should we read and preach on Ascension Day? How much of the evangelists' apocalyptic fervor belongs in the lectionary? The church continues its struggle over the centuries and within the committees about which texts best proclaim God's good news.

1 Timothy 2:15

For we read the texts not as ancient curiosities, stories from the dim past about a religious man, but rather as gospel, as God's liberating news for the community today. The church believes that the books of Matthew, Mark, Luke and John are more than the memoirs of four men. Although there has been a tradition of drawing or sculpting European-looking men as representations of the four evangelists, far more common in the church's liturgical life has been the depictions of the evangelists as the four mysterious beasts. The beasts have a long history as symbolic images of God's power. In the ancient Near East it was usual to flank the throne of the monarch with sculptures of winged beasts, lions or oxen, who represented the extraordinary power of the king. The Israelites borrowed this image when crafting the altar for the tabernacle and again for the temple, for they understood the altar to be the throne of God. The winged beasts who surround the throne of God later appear to Ezekiel in a vision: The two cherubim have become four, each of which has four wings and four faces, of a human, a lion, an ox and an eagle. Also in John's apocalpytic visions, the four living creatures surround the throne. Now each winged beast has a single face—there is a lion, an ox, a human being and an eagle—but countless eyes:

Exodus 25:18–20
Kings 6:23–28

Ezekiel 1:5–14

Revelation 4:6–8

46

"full of eyes in front and behind," "full of eyes all around and within." By the way, both the Hebrew of Ezekiel and the Greek of the Revelation refer to a human face, not to a male face, the history of art notwithstanding.

Already in the second century the four living creatures are seen as representing the four gospels. Irenaeus writes in "Against Heresies" that there must be four gospels, just as there are four corners of the earth and four winds in the sky. And these four gospels are, like the four beasts, images of the activity of the Son of God. There are the princely lion, the sacrificial ox, the human guise and the brooding eagle: "Now the gospels, in which Christ is enthroned, are like these," argues that early defender of the faith. Many's the lectionary cover or frontispiece with depictions of a lion, an ox, a human being and an eagle in its four quadrants. The eagle came to be associated with John, and since medieval times some churches honored the fourth gospel by sculpting an eagle form into the lectern. In my college chapel, mosaics of the living creatures adorn the legs of the altar.

The point, of course, is that the four gospels are recognized as four different faces of the salvation of God. We cannot look on the face of God, but we can look into the faces of the evangelical witnesses, who are mysterious living creatures surrounding God's presence, beasts proclaiming and praising God's salvation, mythical beings flying between God and humankind. Their countless eyes see both the human condition and divine mercy more clearly than we. Their eyes, all around and within, form the eyes of the church. So during the week, Christian scholars learn the original languages to get closer to the evangelists and study the origins of the gospels, their cultural matrix and the history of the transmission of the text to understand more clearly their religious viewpoints. And then on Sunday morning, to acclaim the mystery of God's word among us, to share in the evangelists' sight, to honor the good tidings they bring, we all stand for the reading of the gospel.

To us, O God, you come
with the lion's nobility,
with the eagle's nurture,
to be sacrificed like an ox,
to show us a human face,
four wings to soar beyond the land,
countless eyes to see into all things.
Come, O God, and save us:
Bring us good news.

7

Communion of Saints

Traveling south through Christian Europe, one walks a trail of bones. In Aachen's cathedral treasury are various body remnants enshrined in bejeweled golden reliquaries. One peeks through a glass opening in an ornate Gothic container, and there is part of a femur. In northern Italy we get entire skeletons in glass side altars. Bones here, bones there. In Varese there is a bunkbed altar, with the bones of a virgin martyr below, and a wax model of her above, looking for all the world like Snow White awaiting the prince in the dwarves' glass coffin.

In Milan the skeleton of Ambrose is bedecked in damask vestments, but in spite of the miter one can see the skull that once protected such a brilliant mind: all those hymns and lectures on the sacraments and sermons coming from inside that skull. Moving along from history to myth, Venetian tourists gather around some bones purported to be Mark's, the dubious legend saying more about ecclesiastical power than pious reverence. And back in southern Germany, in a town cemetery, are the bones of Wilhelm Loehe, pastor of a backwater Lutheran parish, who wrote brilliantly on the meaning of the liturgy. On his tombstone are the German words, "I believe in the communion of saints."

For that must be what all these bones are about: the desire to surround oneself with the saints, the need to be in communion with the great and holy folk of the past. Communion: to be at one with. Saints: those brought through baptism to God. *Koinonia ton hagion*: the participation in the holy things. Perhaps it was actually the apostles' bones that started the relic collections, although some of those stories are sheer fantasy. We know that the bones of the early martyrs were reverenced to honor their testimony. Soon enough the game began: Our bones are better than your bones. Most likely some princes who sided with

Martin Luther were already itching to get back at a neighboring bishop for touting a better bone collection.

But there was deep piety for many of the faithful. For an illiterate laity, surrounded by brutality, distanced from priestly power, ignorant of the meaning of the liturgy, and communing only once a year, the skeletons or the skulls (Catherine of Siena's head is in one place, the rest of her bones elsewhere) were a touch of holiness. Reverencing the bones was a way, by approaching a saint, to come near to God.

Finally, the trail of bones leads only to death. It is not surprising that these boneyard churches are filled with depictions of the death of Christ: morbid crucifixions, deposition paintings, one Pietá after another, the weeping women. For me it ended at a glass side altar in which was, believe it or not, a wax image of the dead Jesus. I think: Jesus, a dead Jew. This is Germany and Italy, and I remember walking in the woods by the Mosel River and coming upon an abandoned Jewish cemetery. The last burial was of a Mrs. Simon in 1938. There is a marker noting the deaths in 1942—only the year is given—of her two sons.

I do not mean to say that we ought to forget the saints' burial sites or desecrate the bones of the faithful. I lit a candle by good old Ambrose's remains and prayed for writers in the church. For to be near the bones is a comfort, a primitive link to power, the hope for life beyond death. I too laid wildflowers on my grandparents' graves, attempting to commune with them once again, and I walked the blocks from Princeton University to place evergreens on Jonathan Edwards' tombstone. It is surely a monstrous disorientation of urban life that the cemetery is so distanced from the apartment, the office and the stores that such a communion with the saints is uncommon. Long ago in some

country places where the church stood encircled by the cemetery (well named "the churchyard"), the congregation processed
outside after a baptism to pour out the water on a far plot in the
cemetery, thus to consecrate with baptismal water the infant's
final resting place. To honor the baptized dead: This is a good
and holy thing.

Yet we need other images than bones to depict the commu-
nion of saints. We must have images of the life of the baptized.
In the Mary chapel of the Beuron Benedictine community,
mosaics of Eve, Miriam, Judith, Hannah, all those women of
God, encircle us with the community of saintly souls who like
Mary were signs of God's grace. In the Basilica of St. Apollinare
Nuovo in Ravenna, the procession of holy men flanks one side
of the nave, the procession of holy women the other, marching
up with us to the table, giving praise to God. The cathedral in
Venice is covered from the baseboards to the ceiling peak with
mosaics of the lives of the Hebrew and Christian saints surrounding the bread and wine with us. In the dark womb-church
of Taizé, candles illumine the faces on the icons, and in our
prayer we know ourselves to be in the communion of saints. I
recall my young daughters, accustomed to a starkly modern
church of white walls and butcher block furnishings, tracing
with their small fingertips the bronze reliefs of Elizabeth Seton
and Kateri Tekakwitha on the great doors of St. Patrick Cathedral, mystically communing with two women of our Christian
past. Although letting religious artists loose on sanctuary walls
has sometimes led to liturgical monstrosities, we must think
anew about how to enliven our worship space with images of
the saints.

For to be Christian is never to be alone. "Christian" is not
my given name, but our family name, our adoption surrounding

us with so great a cloud of witnesses. In *The Rhythm of God*, Geddes MacGregor tells of a priest who asked, "How many people were at the early celebration of the eucharist last Wednesday morning?" He replied, "There were three old ladies, the janitor, several thousand archangels, a large number of seraphim, and several million of the triumphant saints of God." Some of the saints are the suffering martyrs whose trials are understood triumphantly in the light of Christ's resurrection. Some of the saints are the victorious faithful whose successes inspire us to holier living. Some are the Catherines who, seeing visions, took on emperor and pope; and some are the Gregorys, lauded for their leadership. Others are the baptized millions whom we commemorate namelessly on All Saints' Day. We seek their company, alive or dead, and we attend their bones in symbolic gesture, a speechless ovation for their legacy.

The church means more by its phrase "the communion of saints" than our constructing lively Mary chapels. For always the church is talking about God. The communion of saints, our participation in the holy — this language is also a description of God, a metaphor for the divine. Traditional Christianity speaks easily of God's transcendence. We know God to be the prime mover of creation and the mighty one of liberation, a God of power and might outside of time and space. But God is also Holy Spirit, an immanent divinity, the absolute might of creation and salvation among us now, the life of Christ in this community here. Feminist Christians know this well, weary of only an elderly father in the sky and a struggling man back then. Here in this assembly of faith is God the Holy Spirit, in this holy catholic church, in this forgiveness of sins, in this communion of saints. The images of the saints enliven our worship spaces by being depictions of God incarnate in the body of the faithful.

The communion of saints is an image of God's very self. It is not that we need to create communion, feverishly shaping manipulative liturgies that foster feelings of unity. There is in baptism already the communion which is God. Of course we can't see it: Whoever said we could see God? We see the sun, a sign of God; we honor the mystery of the cross; we tell the tale of God's backside. But also in the communion of saints is God hidden. Where do we find God? We look and see the old woman saying her rosary at another Italian bone pile, the custodian tending the votive candles at Ambrose's tomb, the Lutheran sister chattering away instead of giving us directions to Loehe's grave. By participation in the holy things we all join in God. We gather round the font; we attend the readings; we stand together to pray; we share in one loaf and one cup; we take food to the hungry. By such participation in the holy things we are made a sign of God.

Philip, speaking for the apostles, asks Jesus when they will get to see God. Jesus replies, "Have I been with you so long, and yet you do not know me?" We smugly think that unlike Philip *John 14:8–9* we would have recognized God's Spirit breathing in our face. But there are those Sundays when we question whether any self-respecting deity would sink so low as to be manifested in stumbling lectors, bumbling presiders, unprepared homilists, cardboard bread, obstructionist committees, lukewarm parishioners, uncaring hierarchy. Suddenly we feel kin to Philip, for it is not easy to see God's Spirit in such as this.

We are in good company with our doubts. Not even Jesus' disciples anticipated a manifestation of God on Golgotha. They forsook Jesus and fled. But they assembled on the first day, and on the eighth day, and in this communion of saints they came to know the risen Lord. Like Thomas we doubt, and like Thomas

John 20:26–29 we touch the wounds of Christ at the eighth day's assembly. The New Testament does not expend energy describing the body of the resurrected Jesus, but it lists the primitive community of *Acts 1:12–14* saints by name. Hippolytus, a second-century saint, taught us to pray, "Gather into one all who share this bread and wine." So in this gathering we are one with the saints; our communion is in Christ, and so we are brought to God.

O Holy Spirit of God,
your breath rings us round.
Your blood enlivens our bones,
and all the saints, dead and alive,
commune in you.
Come, Holy Spirit,
fill the hearts of the faithful,
and animate in us the body of Christ.

Prayer

The book of 1 Kings tells a lively story of the power of prayer. *1 Kings 18:20–40* The people of Israel are shilly-shallying between worship of the LORD, the God of the exodus, and worship of Baal and Asherah, the Canaanite deities. Elijah proposes a contest: Both sides are to pray for the gift of divine fire, and whichever deity responds appropriately will be acclaimed victorious. So the Baal worshipers construct an altar, set out the sacrificial bull, call out their petitions, perform a ritual dance and slash themselves in a bloodletting that surely will evoke divine blessing. But it is useless, says this confident Hebrew story. Elijah eggs them on: Perhaps Baal is napping, he suggests, or, using a Hebrew phrase that few translations render accurately, out relieving himself! But when Elijah, pouring water three times over his bull, offers a brief prayer of faith, divine fire bursts from the heavens and consumes the bull, the stone altar and all the water as well. All Israel acclaims the LORD as God and promptly slaughters the 450 prophets of Baal.

The glorious court legend of Jehoshaphat makes the same point. Jehoshaphat's massive army, which the chronicler claims *2 Chronicles 20:1–29* had over a million soldiers, does not even have to fight in the *2 Chronicles 17:12–19* victorious battle against the invaders from Moab and Ammon. The king merely instructs the Levites to sing a psalm, and the enemy is routed.

"Give thanks to the LORD, whose steadfast love endures forever," chant the Levites. Those words are the refrain in many *2 Chronicles 20:21* psalms which praise the God who answers prayer. Perhaps it was Psalm 107 they sang, in which wanderers are brought home, prisoners granted freedom, the sick awarded health and the storm-tossed a haven; the desert becomes a paradise and the needy turn wealthy. For they all "cried to the LORD in their distress," and their every prayer is answered. Perhaps it was Psalm 136 that

Jehoshaphat ordered, in which God is praised for creating the world, overthrowing Pharaoh and toppling Canaanite kings.

These stories make for better entertainment than theology. For we know all too well the countless times that the faithful believers did not succeed in invoking divine fire from heaven. Like the Canaanite prophets, we know the endless ritual pleading which appears to bring no divine intervention. We do not believe that our prayer is as powerful as Elijah's petition and Jehoshaphat's psalm. We see no fire, we enjoy no victory, and our enemies are not destroyed at the end of the ordeal.

Luke 11:1 "Teach us to pray," the disciples said.

1 Samuel 1:9–11 Sometimes like Hannah we try to make a deal with God: If you open my womb and give me a son, I'll give the son back to *Judges 16:23–31* you. Sometimes like Samson we offer to do God a favor: If you return my strength to me this last time, I'll destroy more evil than in the whole rest of my life put together. Sometimes like *Numbers 11:10–24* Moses we complain about our lot: This wilderness trek wasn't my idea, so why do I have to deal with all its problems? Sometimes, *Genesis 18:22–32* feeling generous, we join Abraham in interceding for others: Should the whole city be destroyed because of only a few who *Jonah 4:1–3* are wicked? More often, feeling testy, we gripe with Jonah that the evil do not appear to be getting their just desserts.

"Teach us to pray," the disciples said.

Surely, we hope, when the insiders pray, an answer will *Mark 4:35–39* come. The disciples pray for safety in the storm and are saved. Yet the New Testament tells us surprising stories. The Roman centurion prays for his paralyzed servant. "Lord, I am not wor- *Matthew 8:5–13* thy," he said, and oppressor that he is, his prayer is answered. *Matthew 15:21–28* The Canaanite woman begs health for her daughter, and Jesus grants this request, though she is a Canaanite, though she is a

woman. And there is the thief on the cross, who will be remem-   *Luke 23:42–43*
bered on the last and great day.

"Teach us to pray," the disciples said.

For we have come to the place in the liturgy when we pray. As Justin wrote in 150 when describing Christian worship, "Then we all stand up together and offer prayers." We have prayed the short prayer of the day before the readings, and we will pray the great thanksgiving at the table, but here is the intercessory prayer, when we put words to all the longings of our hearts. But for what shall we long? There were times when this prayer was suppressed, and communities where this prayer was prescribed, but now we expect it to be newly composed, perhaps by the parish itself, to have some relation to the week's events, to be informed by the readings or the season. Whether the whole prayer or several petitions for it, we are writing prayers.

"Hear our prayer."

On any given Sunday a vast array of texts pass themselves off as intercessory prayer. Shall we stereotype them? There is the rehash of the homily, which coerces the congregation to ascribe to the tenets of the preacher, like it or not. There is the medita-tion on the lessons, which weaves the language of the readings into a poem-like reverie. There is the parish bulletin board, in which last week's crises and this week's events are announced before God's face. There is the exercise in consciousness-raising, the "help-us-to-realize" prayer, through which particular social and political views are inculcated. There is the activists' prayer, sometimes bordering on atheist prayer, in which not God but human beings are asked to solve the problems of the world. Some petitions are too convoluted to be understood, some too dull to be endured.

The tradition has attempted to guide the church into this prayer with a simple maxim: In the intercessions the community prays for the needs of others. We focus not primarily on our needs, nor on an application of the text to ourselves. In this prayer we focus on those who are not present: on the entire church of God, the created world, the nations of the earth, the community in which we reside, those absent from our company because of sickness or troubling circumstances.

This prayer trains the faithful to have their heart with others, especially those in ill fortune. While contemporary psychology urges us to know our own hearts and solve our own problems, Christian ethics calls us to live as if our hearts are not set full and complete in our own bodies, but are always half with those in need. There is an African language in which to say "John is sick," one says "We are sick in John." If there is a single biblical image of intercessory prayer, it is the wedding of Cana, *John 2:2* when Mary says to Jesus, "They have no wine."

Week after week, year after year, century after century, the faithful have prayed for the peace, justice, sustenance and health of the world. "Hear our prayer. Hear our prayer. Hear our prayer." This continual praying is evidence of the faith of the church that God has acted, is acting, will act, to bring life to the world. I wonder: Do you suppose the state of the world would be worse than it is if these intercessions were to stop? If the prayers seem to no avail, the faithful simply pray more. The widow in the Lucan parable keeps on pestering the judge for vindication of her cause, and finally the unjust judge acts in her favor merely to *Luke 18:1–7* be rid of her. So like the widow we keep hammering away on the doors of God's bounty.

We want to believe that in God is boundless life for the whole creation, and so we lament the death around us and plead for God's creative spirit to brood again over the chaos, restoring *shalom*. We want to train our hearts to be with the needy, and so we give this part of the liturgy to those needier than ourselves. We want to temper our deathly individualism with the Christian ideal that, bound together in love, we have no peace unless others have peace. The last sentence Martin Luther wrote, scribbled on the paper by his deathbed, was not a last will and testament like "I was the center of the century's greatest social and religious upheaval," but simply the phrase, "We are beggars, this is true." The church is the body which begs that God's generosity will enliven all the begging world.

It is not easy to keep this up, week after week, decade after decade. Perhaps some Sundays, some years, some of us don't believe anymore that this prayer can effect anything. It seems as if Elijah's taunt is a possibility, that our god is out relieving himself. Fortunately, during those weeks, someone else believes and keeps the prayer going: "Hear our prayer. Hear our prayer. Hear our prayer." And the intercessions for the church, the world, the community, and those absent pull God back to the business of saving the world and pull us back to compassion and faith.

The stories say that you listen,
the saints say that you answer.
O God, whom we call omnipotent,
O God, whom we name compassionate,
hear our prayer,
receive our prayer,
let our cry come to you.
For we are beggars, this is true.

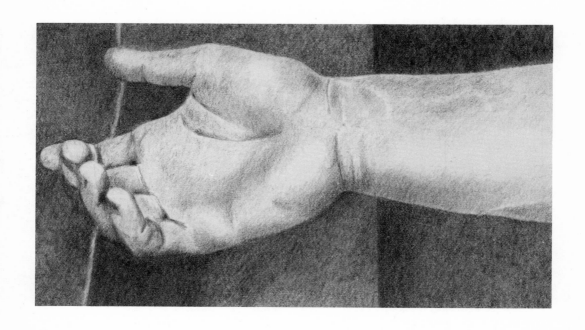

Offer

Open the door of the simple verb "to offer," and you find rooms and corridors, stairways and closets to investigate. There is the ancient and ever-present human longing to connect with the divine; there are complex biblical usages and polemical theological debates; and underneath the scholarly analysis of the verb lies the ever-shifting metaphoric meaning. In fact, few words in the liturgy better illustrate the nature of Christian metaphoric speech. Let us begin to explore this mysterious mansion.

Religion is replete with offering. The more archeological digs, the more discoveries of rituals, the longer grows the list of examples: Human beings find ways to present gifts to their deities. Perhaps humans wish to make a trade with the deities: If we give one of our herd, or the first bushel of the harvest, the god will continue to send the rain, the goddess will continue to bless the wheat field. Perhaps the deities are justifiably—or inexplicably—enraged at humankind, and gifts of appeasement are indicated. Perhaps the deities smile on mortals, and welcome a meal which because it rises to the heavens in smoke can magically connect the human with the divine.

More brutal theories satisfy the Freudian-minded among us. Perhaps the deepest and most pervasive human activity is violence, and communities channeled this violent activity into pious rituals of social cohesion; eventually the bloody sacrifices were understood as being offered to the gods and goddesses. To make the study of ancient religion more confusing, few rituals clearly indicate one specific meaning. Our categories—this is Offering Type A, that is Offering Type B—only partially account for this archetypal human activity.

Study of the Hebrew Scriptures indicates that also in the Bible are different kinds of offerings to God. Later meanings are interwoven with earlier sagas: Urban scribes who knew well a certain temple sacrifice use some of their own language to describe the offerings of nomadic tribes hundreds of years before. It is complicated to sort out. Sometimes the offerings are tied to praise and communion, other times to guilt and expiation, yet other times to vows and obligations. Over the centuries Israelites offered to God animals burned wholly as well as animals slaughtered for a meal shared by God, the priest and the devotee. Cereal, firstfruits, incense were offered. And although Abraham is stopped from offering his beloved son, Hannah does complete her offering, presenting her weaned toddler Samuel to the priest at the shrine in gratitude to God for the gift of fertility.

Genesis 22:1–14

1 Samuel 1:21–28

Theologians debate: What did all this mean? The most ancient tales come down to us without explication, and the prophets whose logic is more clear were highly critical of these ritual offerings. Many theologians judge that usually the offering functioned as a symbol of religious devotion. The offering was the external expression of people's response to God. Whether the worshiper felt dependence, guilt, gratitude or desire, the offering externalized the internal state. Of course, the internal state could exist before God's face quite without the external sign. The prophets suggest that the sacrifices of animals and foodstuffs are metaphors of our state of being, and if our state of being is not the appropriate religious devotion, the sacrifice is a metaphor of nothing.

Let's run down another corridor. The truth is that Christian use of "offering" is more complicated even than in tribal religions or Israelite ritual. For from at least the end of the first century, Christians used the language of offering to explicate the meaning of the crucifixion. Christ "gave himself up for us, a fragrant offering and sacrifice to God," writes the author of

Ephesians. Although neither the evangelists nor Paul develops *Ephesians 5:2* this metaphor, the letter to the Hebrews is almost wholly a treatise on "offering." There is no more need of regular cultic offerings, for Christ is the offering. We are so accustomed to this metaphor that we forget how odd it is. Hebrews gives us an astounding juxtaposition: Jesus Christ, the itinerant teacher who was executed, is like a high priest who offers a sacrifice, the sacrifice being himself. Our corridor just took a right-angle turn, and we can no longer see the light back in the foyer.

Some early apologists played with the metaphor of offering. Justin writes to the emperor, who is familiar with religious processions preceding sacrifices to the deities, that the way Christians "conduct religious processions" is by giving thanks and sharing food. The way Christians offer God food is that at each assembly they take up a collection for the needy. The mosaics in Ravenna's San Vitale depict Abel with his lamb, Melchizedek with his bread, Abraham at table with the three visitors, Abraham at the altar with Isaac, and the Empress Theodora with a jeweled chalice. Each of these images expresses a different variation on the metaphor of offering.

But it was not long before the metaphor became literalized. Presiders were understood to be genuine priests who offered actual sacrifices in the stead of the unworthy lay petitioners. Christ was the offering, and the priest had the power to present this sacrifice to God. Ancient practices of ritual purity before the sacrifice came to determine clerical identity and life-style. But this rigid literalizing did not bend and breathe, as metaphors do, and the language broke apart. Martin Luther, newly drawn to the biblical sources and critical of medieval clerical traditions, aimed a good deal of his vitriolic disputations at the way the church had come to use the language of offering, and for several centuries the Reformation churches indulged in their own rigid and literal use of the language of offering.

The language of offering is very much with us. The Roman Catholic liturgy speaks of the bread and wine we are given to offer and of the sacrifice the priest offers. Lutherans sing of offering a sacrifice of thanksgiving. Episcopalians cite biblical passages about offering during their offertory. Methodists offer themselves and their gifts, Presbyterians present the offerings of their life and labor. The language of the Roman church suggests that the priest offers the bread and wine, while the ritual of the Protestant churches, with the minister raising high toward heaven the "offering baskets," counters that the people offer their money. The denominational differences, faithfully representing historic emphases, do not surprise us.

But all the churches "offer" metaphorically. The sacrificial connotation of "offer" does not literally apply to these actions: our reminding God and ourselves of the martyrdom of Christ, our setting out bread and wine, our collection of money for the poor and for church maintenance, our praising God. Even most tithers in affluent America are stretching it to imply that theirs is "sacrificial giving." "Offer" is an exaggeration, the wrong word, an image oddly superimposed, a metaphor.

Thomas Aquinas trained Christian theologians to agree with Aristotle that metaphors are not only suspect but extraneous. The Western mind hoped that accuracy of labeling was possible, and Aquinas was particularly wary when the odd elaboration found in metaphoric speech was applied to God. But contemporary linguistic philosophers have disagreed with our eminent forefathers on this issue. In *The Rule of Metaphor*, Paul Ricoeur ably demonstrates that far from being unnecessary decoration, metaphor is the supreme activity of the human mind.

Metaphoric speech perceives the world creatively by juxtaposing the known with the unknown. After metaphor, reality is seen anew. Without metaphor we could not express human emotion, share religious experience with others or describe God at all. The fact that God is wholly other requires human beings to use metaphor in their religious speech.

So the language of offering is here to stay. Not that like pious Hindus we set out food by the lingam that Siva may eat. But, religious creatures that we are, we want to present gifts to God. We bring bread and wine for the meal, and we allot time, money and energy for the good of others; and we call these offerings, external signs of our internal state of praise and thanksgiving. Recalling "As you have done it to one of the least," we give food to God by feeding the poor. Believing that in the bread and wine is Christ, we offer God remembrance and renewal of the offering of Jesus.

Matthew 25:40

But for the metaphor to stay alive, we must continually recognize it as metaphor. There is no bloody sacrifice here. There is not usually any deprivation of life, no burning up of a valued possession. (Remember Scarlet in *Gone With the Wind* "giving up" for the cause of the confederacy the wedding band of the man she never loved, merely to show up sweet Melanie?) Our food for the meal with God, our share of the expense of church maintenance, our gifts for the poor are like offerings and, true to the ambiguity of metaphor, are not like offerings. We do not offer, says the prophet, the fruit of our body for the sin of our soul. Rather, we show kindness and do justice.

Micah 6:7

As if God needs our offerings! In some religions the deities do require offerings, or they demonstrate their gratitude for receiving such gifts by showering down blessings. But Christians have said that God is not contingent on humanity. The Trinity is wholly loving in itself and needs no creation, no humankind, to fulfill its needs and complete its being. That Christians offer gifts to God proves that we are humans; that God does not require any offerings proves that God is God. Ah, and if we collect money to pay for resurfacing the church's parking lot, is this an offering to God?

It's been a long exploration through the offering-house. (Does the parking lot count as part of the mansion?) "Offer" is an is-and-is-not word, usually not factual, sometimes not even true. But it is part of the clothing we wear to the wedding feast, our ancient priestly garb hidden inside our dresses and jeans and *Exodus 28:33–34* albs. The golden bells on the robe of Aaron are ringing in our ears as the Smith family walks up the aisle carrying bread and *Psalm 51:19* wine, the smoke from a burning bull filling our nostrils as we sing the Holy, Holy.

I'm home from school, here is my picture,
take it, Mama.
We're back from camp, here is a bookmark,
take it, Papa.
If I get well, I'll serve you all my days,
please, Almighty One.

One offering or another
to you, benevolent God:
Smile on us with divine forebearing.

Give Thanks

The first Thanksgiving at Plymouth Plantation is legendary for citizens of the United States. The first winter of 1620 had killed off over half of the 102 passengers of the Mayflower. But the survivors were celebrating their first harvest with enough fowl to feast for a week, and the 90 native guests, along with their chief, Massasoit, contributed five deer to the festival of peace and plenty. The scene was not as dour as we had thought, for we know now that our image of grey- and black-attired pilgrims with white platter collars and broad cuffs was an invention of a nineteenth-century artist. Rather, these colorfully clad folk, having escaped disease and despair, engaged in that archetypal human activity: They rendered thanksgiving to their deity at a harvest festival.

It is a pity that this myth gets lost amidst ignoble tales of the slaughter of the American Indians and of squatters' rights. The American expectation of getting what we want too easily overwhelms the habit of thanksgiving. Thank-you notes are becoming passé. Youth are excused monstrously ungrateful behavior. Pop psychology encourages private feelings rather than social dictates, and thus more occasions for expressions of gratitude are abandoned. For we Americans tend to believe that life, liberty and happiness, far from being gracious gifts from God, are the inalienable rights of our revolutionary ardor, or, perhaps, benefits due to those consumers who can pay for them.

Scripture would have us live otherwise: Oh, but not with dozens of stories of our grateful ancestors in the faith. In fact, there are sorrowfully few narratives of faithful folk who, in gratefulness for specific benefits received or for the continual blessings of their life, render thanksgiving to God. We ought not be surprised; people were the same then as now. There we are, the nine Judeans reprimanded in Luke, who when cured of leprosy,

hurry off to get back to our lives without first giving thanks
Luke 17:12–19 to the one who healed them. To give thanks would be to admit
our need, our dependency on God. It is more modern to join
with Job's visitors and claim that people get either the evil or
Job 4, 5, 8, 10 the good they deserve.

But what the scriptures do demonstrate is that thanksgiving, while not being a normal human response, is the habit for
worship. The Hebrew author of Chronicles, intent on establish-
ing the idea that under King David the people were faithful
worshipers of the LORD, records over and over that the Levites
sang thanksgivings in the sacred tent. The psalms, written down
because they were used in corporate worship, are filled with
thanksgivings: The earth has yielded a good harvest, the sick
have been returned to health, the nation's enemies have been
vanquished, and so all the people give thanks. It is as if corporate worship teaches us to give thanks, puts thanksgiving into
the mouths of us ungrateful wretches, and so forms us in a habit
of gratitude.

It is this habit of gratitude that Paul urges on the young
Christian communities with his repeated call that we give
thanks. It is this habit of gratitude that Justin writes of, when he
describes the eucharist as the primary example of the entire
Christian life of always giving thanks. This same habit of gratitude helps Perpetua, the young African martyr of the third
century, to cry out in prison, "Thanks be to God."

Thanksgiving is, as it were, the Christian way of life, and
the primary worship service of Christians trains us in such a pattern of living. At the start of the new week, we gather to give
thanks. Justin writes that the presider "gives thanks at some
length," and again, that he "offers prayers and thanksgiving to
the best of his ability." This service of thanksgiving has been

titled many ways: the Lord's Supper, the Table of the Lord, Holy Communion, the Breaking of the Bread, the Divine Liturgy, Mass. But the ancient name for the weekly event, a name newly popular in ecumenical conversation, is the Greek word meaning thanksgiving: eucharist. *Eucharistomen:* Let us give thanks, we say in English. *Eucharistomen:* We pray "at some length" our thanksgivings.

And of course we do not always feel like it. Ill, lonely, upset, discouraged, at least tired, perhaps hung over, we would not on our own be thankful every Sunday morning. But to be Christian is to choose the habit of thanksgiving and to join with other Christians to cultivate the habit. Here's a reason to attend the Sunday liturgy: not because we have to, not only when we want to, but to train ourselves in thanksgiving.

In the first part of the Great Thanksgiving we situate ourselves. Perhaps that very morning we had staggered to church, hardly conscious of the date, far from praise. Yet the preface sets our morning praise in its proper place in the year's cycle of thanksgiving. We may have felt lonely and isolated; yet the prayer states that our voices in this sanctuary join with those of all Christians living and dead. During the prior days we may have been keenly aware of our pitiable human weakness, but this thanksgiving declares that our human voices blend with those of the choirs of angels. We are caught up in the church's thanksgiving, beside the angels' thanksgiving, our whimpers transformed into gratitude.

We give thanks for creation. Taught by the Jews to give thanks to the Sovereign of the ages for the whole created order, some eucharistic prayers are full of praise for the benevolent universe. We believe, not like Deists that God created the universe eons ago and is now in retirement, but rather that God continuously creates the world, sending the rain, tending the crops, feeding the people. The creation story of Genesis 1 describes the world as a perfectly designed and wondrously good home for humankind, and inspired by this story Christians give thanks.

We give thanks for salvation. Faithful Jews give thanks that they have been chosen, faithful Christians that they have been saved. For both peoples, that which grants them identity is recognized as a gift from God for which they render thanks. God has freed the slaves and brought them into freedom; God has lived and died among us to bring us peace. Both Jews and Christians acknowledge the very course of human history to be the arena for divine mercy. Human life is all too often experienced as one damn thing after another; the life of thanksgiving, quite the contrary, praises God for one blessing after another.

We give thanks for God's promises. Even our prayers for the gifts of the Spirit, for the unity of the church, and for the coming of God's dominion are petitions in the spirit of thanksgiving. Like the Jews shouting "Next year in Jerusalem!" we too dare to cry out for God's dominion because of the covenant of God's promises to us. We stand now as Christ's body in the world. In us is God's Spirit, and in gratefulness for that Spirit we pray for its continued power in the world. To live in ingratitude would be to deny that very Spirit in which we live.

We know that at least since the year 215 Christians have engaged in that dialogue so familiar to us:

> The Lord be with you,
> And also with you.
> Lift up your hearts,
> We have them with the Lord.
> Let us give thanks to the Lord,
> It is fitting and right.

We know as well from early Christian art that the posture of this praise was the *orans* position. Not only the presider, but the entire community stood with arms upraised to offer thanksgiving. All together gave thanks, all together practiced praise. Can we begin again to adopt the stance of the presider praising together with hands upraised?

Over the centuries the culture overwhelmed this radical expression of a single people standing in praise. Western Christianity found itself bifurcated and morose, one man speaking intercessions for mercy while the people knelt in private devotion: the presider distant, his mercy remote, and thanksgiving forgotten. Historians catalog all the conditions that led to this decline, but to their impressive list we must add also this human truth: Given the miseries of human life, thanksgiving is unbelievable. It easily yields to other states of mind unless we self-consciously practice its posture and tone. It wilts without watering. It starves without the feast.

But thanksgiving must be more and other than merely the optimism of the middle- and upper-class, the manners of folk who have never missed a meal and thus live in profound untruth if they live ungratefully. And Karl Marx has shamed us into admitting that the song of thanksgiving cannot be the mesmerizing mantra of those whose days are filled with misery and pain. Thanksgiving is not a personal emotion, based on the situation of the moment. Rather, thanksgiving is the belief of the whole people of God assembled in the Spirit. It is our faith in the providence of God; it is our shared life in God's beneficence.

To sing together "Let us give thanks" is to speak a succinct creed. The phrase implies a belief in God, a view of creation and an attitude toward human history; upon these rest the commensurate life-style of gratitude. By being cast in the plural, the phrase corrects our tendency to self-sufficiency with the religious truth of interdependence, and by being thanksgiving, the phrase makes us complainers rise anew in praise.

We lift our hearts
—our arms so woefully heavy—
O cornucopia God.

We give you thanks,
"not as we ought
but as we are able,"

We lift our hearts,
in joyful effort
to offer thanksgiving.

God of Power and Might

A 1480 Book of Hours is opened to the feast day of St. Michael and All Angels. The antiphon, *"Michael archangele veni in adjutorium populi dei,"* is illuminated with a depiction of Michael, wearing an alb, stole and brocade cope, boasting massive golden wings and luxuriant golden curls, and brandishing a sword over five bestial demons who look rather like kindergarten monkeys squirming away from their teacher. The castle in the background is secure, confident in the angel's protection. God's power and might conquer evil, and the victory is wreathed by an intricate border of leaves and vines, flowers and birds, a filigree of creation framing salvation.

We are accustomed to such illustrations of God's power and might, although usually not so splendid as this tiny painting with Michael a beautiful being, a powerful warrior and a vested priest all at once. We are instead plagued with angels as simpering ghosts, weak dreams of Victorian godliness, or as cuddly toddlers looking more like flying piglets than the fingers of God. That is one thing that the scriptures understand angels to be: the powerful hands of God, the agents of divine might.

It is as the mighty arm of God that an angel with a flaming sword bars access to the tree of life, an angel stays Abraham's knife so that Isaac is saved, angels descend from heaven to bless the sleeping Jacob, an angel appears to Moses from the flames of the burning bush, an angel feeds Elijah bread in the wilderness. When the three strangers dine with Abraham at Mamre and promise Sarah a son, the narrative interchangeably calls the visitors men, angels and the LORD. In the ancient stories, humans receive the salvation of God through the hands of an angel.

Genesis 3:24

Genesis 22:11

Genesis 28:12–13

Exodus 3:2
1 Kings 19:5

Genesis 18:1–16; 19:1

Then come narratives of Israel at war. The people are slaves, then conquerers, then again the vanquished, and they plead for the angelic intervention of God's power and might. An

Exodus 14:19
Judges 6:11–16
angel guards the people of Israel against the advancing Egyptians, and an angel calls Gideon into battle. The angels come to be understood as the heavenly army, the hosts of God fighting for Israel. The highly imaginative books written by Jews in the several centuries before Christ include copious descriptions of the nine ranks of angelic forces, with archangels as commanders, readying themselves for the ultimate battle against evil. To this oppressed and enslaved people, the warring hosts of God's angels were the outstretched arm of God's power and might.

Before the word "hosts" conjured up the image of angelic armies, "hosts" was a name ancient Near Eastern peoples gave the planets and stars. Israel's neighbors worshiped "the host of 2 Kings 17:16 heaven," as do astrologers today, seeing in the movements of the heavenly bodies signs of divine power and messages from the might of the universe. The Hebrew scriptures tell of Manasseh, a particularly impious king of Judah, who allowed worship of the god Baal and the goddess Asherah, and who himself honored 2 Kings 21:3 "all the host of heaven." But the prophets claimed that the LORD was God of the hosts of heaven, God above Baal and Asherah, God who created and governed the heavenly bodies.

We Christians preserve and continue this intriguing mixture of convenantal faith and imaginative legend when we sing Isaiah 6:1–6 "Holy, holy, holy." This song comes from Isaiah, in which the prophet is called by a vision of angels in the temple. The temple is suddenly the heavenly court of God, the angels God's courtiers. Seeing this vision of God's majesty, Isaiah confesses his unworthiness and accepts the call to proclaim the word of God. An angel, again the hand of God, touches the prophet's lips with the burning coal, and so Isaiah is enabled to praise.

The angels in this vision praise the "God of Sabaoth," and scholars have long debated whether "Sabaoth," which means "hosts," has roots in the idea of God's ascendency over the planets or over the angelic armies, since both stars and angels are "hosts." Perhaps the two are mingled in the poetic mind: In Job stars are called angels.

Job 38:7

Now for the translators' debate: How shall we cast this image in contemporary American English? The Latin kept the Hebrew: "Dominus Deus Sabaoth," we sang in the old days. "Sabaoth," simply a transliteration of the Hebrew word, was often misunderstood as having something to do with sabbath. "Heavenly host of armies," the scholarly consensus on the word's literal translation, perpetuates a militaristic image of God that is distasteful to many.

Perhaps, suggest the translators, rather than transliteration or translation, we should give a dynamic equivalent, offering the idea in another form. Even in John's Revelation the angels, singing now in Greek, chant "Holy, holy, holy" to God "almighty";

Revelation 4:8

the Hebrew image of heavenly armies has been replaced by the Greek philosophical category of divine omnipotence. Indeed, in translating another Hebrew title for God in Genesis, "El Shaddai," biblical committees have always used the word

Genesis 17:1

"Almighty," although the word does not mean that at all. "El Shaddai," an ancient image, means either "God of the mountain peaks" or "God of the mothering breasts," or both, we know not; the life of the image was lost ages before our text was written. So just as the biblical translators threw up their hands and rendered Shaddai as Almighty, and just as the Greek poet substituted Almighty for the seraphim's Sabaoth, contemporary liturgists have agreed that in our singing of the Sanctus we will praise the "God of power and might."

The decision concerning translation is one conundrum, but the deeper mystery lies in the challenge of faith. What do modern people mean when they praise a God "of power and might"? The omnipotence of God is not a fashionable idea these days, and its relationship to Christianity is questionable. Omnipotence arises from a Greek philosophical inference about divinity, rather than from biblical narratives about God's action in the world. We post-Holocaust Christians contemplate famine and plague, oppression and war, social evil and ecclesiastical stupidity, and we ache for a God of power and might. Yet many Christian intercessory prayers reflect the agnosticism of the age, with petitions urging that the community alter its consciousness rather than that God's power and might re-create the world.

The New Testament counters the comforting idea of divine omnipotence with the scandal of the incarnation. The ancient legends said that Gabriel was the angel whose trumpet would

Daniel 8:15–17

Luke 1:26

usher in the end time, yet Luke writes that Gabriel announced the birth of a baby to a young woman. Hebrew poetry expected the hosts of heaven to proclaim to all creation Israel's trium-

Isaiah 2:2–4

Luke 2:8–12

phant victory, yet Luke records the song of these angels to an audience of poor shepherds. It's a down-scaled God, a God in a manger, a God among the poor, a God on a cross. The powerful and mighty king is crowned with thorns, and we in the liturgy sing this ancient praise along with the Hosanna of the Jerusalem crowds as we assemble around not a throne with its gilt and brocade but a table serving elemental food.

But now tottering on the shoulders of pregnant Mary and betraying Peter is the monstrous superstructure of the church. Our medieval cathedrals shout out their power and might. Our chain of ecclesiastical authority mimics secular models of social dominance. We have forgotten, forgotten, forgotten that the pillars of our church are not the pompous sovereigns of the Middle Ages but the beggars singing of God. In Giotto's fresco in Assisi, Pope Innocent III is sleeping away; his head cannot rest on the pillow, since he is wearing his miter to bed; and yet there in his dream poor Francis is bearing up the floundering church.

The creation and the salvation of God occur neither in primordial acts of power nor in cataclysmic strokes of might. Rather, God's power and might create and save continuously, incarnately, for us. Without expecting omnipotence, we can praise a God who minute by minute broods over the universe, shaping chaos into ordered beauty. We laud our God who daily protects us from the demons always squirming underfoot. We worship a God who created the hosts of heaven, who saves us by joyful might, who reaches out to all the world from this very table with thousands upon thousands of outstretched arms of mercy.

Honor to our earthbound God!
Your power is promise,
your might is mercy.
All the angels' wings are yours.
Shelter us from chaos,
shield us from evil,
and burn us clean with the coal of the cross.

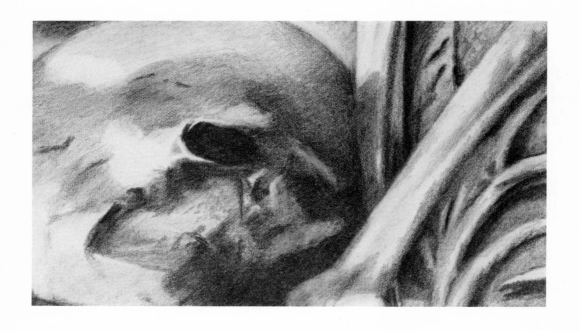

Sanctify

Most religions assume that there is something beyond, above, or within the commonplace. On this deeper or higher level, human life discovers a more profound or noble meaning. Characteristically religions place this deeper or higher level with the divine: A group of divinities, or a single god, or cosmic law, or symbolic action, enriches human life, rescuing it from meaninglessness and death. The religious enterprise hopes to make contact with the divine, to be in the right place when the divine is manifested, so that life might be transformed.

Christianity refers to this idea with the Latin word sanctification. People and things and times are sanctified, rendered sacred, by the power of God. This sanctification, this connecting humanity with divinity, is celebrated or even occasioned in Christian ritual. Persons or time or objects are set apart from their ordinariness in order to be closer to God. The English way to say this idea is "to make holy"—the thousand-year-old word "holy" meaning, of course, not sinless, but whole. To be connected with God is to be made whole. Sanctification makes us what we were intended to be when first formed in the mind of God. Our fragmentation from God, from others in the community, and within ourselves is mended by sanctification. No longer stray pebbles strewn on the walkway, we are now one of the magnificent mosaics in the churches of Ravenna.

When Christians describe sanctification, they cite the work of the Holy Spirit. For life to be made whole, the community invokes the Holy Spirit. When we set someone apart from the world's value struggles for a church career, God's Spirit is invoked. When we honor the dead for their sanctity, we claim to have seen the life of the Spirit in their deeds. For mere water to be the baptismal sign, God's Spirit is invoked. For bread to take its rightful place as the sign of divine life, we "consecrate" the bread. Indeed, a medieval name for the great thanksgiving prayer is "the consecration prayer"—a limited term suggesting that only the bread and wine receive the Spirit of God.

For the Spirit of God enlivens the whole creation. The first creation story in Genesis says that the Spirit of God hovered over the waters like a nesting bird on the primordial cosmic egg.

Genesis 1:2

Psalm 104:29–30

Hebrew poetry links the Spirit with God's breath, and in the second creation story the first human being lives only after

Genesis 2:7

God's Spirit has been breathed into the clay. When God's Spirit is withdrawn, human beings die: So states the odd passage in

Genesis 6:3

Genesis 6 which limits each human life to 120 years.

It is instructive to trace the record of the movement of the Spirit through Hebrew history. When primordial time was over, in the early days of the Israelite people, the Spirit seized extraordinary persons who then charismatically led the people. Pharaoh acknowledged that Joseph has the Spirit of God since he can

Genesis 41:38

interpret dreams. Bezalel received the Spirit of God in order to

Exodus 31:3

design and craft the tabernacle and its glorious furnishings—a reassuring story for all those who shape and fill liturgical space. It is by the Spirit that the military leaders conquer the land of Canaan. Indeed, because he is filled by the Spirit of God,

Judges 11:29

Jepthah destroys 20 cities "with very great slaughter."

Once the Israelites lived more securely in the land, the

1 Samuel 10:10

Spirit was granted to the chosen leader. Saul receives the Spirit,

1 Samuel 16:13

and later David. The kingly anointing with oil signifies the outpouring of God's Spirit. When kings weaken, there are the prophets: Elisha receives twice the Spirit of the LORD that Elijah

2 Kings 2:16

had had. But when all these human leaders fail, the poets plead

Isaiah 11:1–9

for a perfect king, the mythical branch of Jesse, who will speak

Isaiah 61

good tidings and establish peace and vindicate the righteous: On this great one the Spirit of the LORD will rest. Surely the time will come when the Spirit will return to enliven the people.

Luke's writing narrates one early Christian understanding of the coming of God's Spirit. The Spirit comes upon Mary at the annunciation, and upon Jesus at his baptism, that we may know who Jesus is. In the synagogue Jesus claims that the Isaian promise of the coming of the Spirit is that very day, in that very assembly, fulfilled, and later Jesus promises that God will grant the Spirit to any who ask. The Book of Acts chronicles the movement of this Spirit, beginning with the apostolic circle, through the primitive community and out into all the people of the earth. *Luke 1:35* *Luke 3:22* *Luke 4:16–21* *Luke 11:13* *Acts 2*

Luke's excitement that the Spirit of Jesus Christ is spreading throughout the world meets its caveat in the Johannine community. The Johannine epistles laud the presence of the Spirit of Christ in their own communities, but they fervently warn against other groups who erroneously believe that also they have the true Spirit. Already during the first century Christians are quarreling about who and what is sanctified, about who and what is not. *1 John 4:1–6*

It is all too commonplace that religious communities struggle to harness God's Spirit so that their holy people can enjoy exclusive rights to divine power. The archetypal story of this tendency begins with Moses' complaining before God that he has too much work to do and is lonely in his leadership position. The account says that God took some of the divine Spirit that Moses had and redistributed it to the 70 elders whom Moses had chosen. All right and proper. But there were two others, not present at the ritual, found later to be prophesying in the camp! Great consternation ensues: What to do with this Eldad and Medad? But the ground does not open up to swallow these *Numbers 11:10–30*

Numbers 16:31–32
Numbers 12:9–10
upstarts, nor are they struck with leprosy as Miriam was. Moses, in atypical appreciation for the laity, cries out, "Would that all the LORD's people were prophets, that the LORD's Spirit would be given to them all!"

The idea that all the people might be sanctified begins already in the Pentateuch. Despite pages of detailed ritual in Leviticus describing the priests, their consecration, clothing, responsibilities and life-style, the story of the giving of the law at Sinai promises that the whole people will be priests, a holy Exodus 19:6 nation. The public consecration of a few men was only a sign of the mysterious consecration of the whole people. We discover in the New Testament that some leaders in the primitive church, among them Peter, believed that the kosher food laws—which set apart only some food and only some people as fit for the table of God's people—could be maintained. Paul led those who Galatians 2:11–16 believed that the new creation had already begun: All food and all persons have been sanctified by Christ's meals with the outcasts. In Christ, all is kosher.

Moses's wish, that the Spirit would rest upon everyone in the community, underlies much Christian prayer. Would that all the world could be saved! Would that all of life be sanctified by the divine Spirit! Christians see Joel's dream that the Spirit would alight on the whole community as begun at Pentecost but Joel 2:28–29 realized only in the end time, when God will be victorious and the divine Spirit will re-create the whole world. As a child I hesitated praying for the coming of the kingdom, for I imagined it would be the end of all the good I knew. My catechesis had failed to make clear the essential point that the eschaton will be the end only of all the evil we know. We will no longer be separated from God; God will sanctify the world and all will be whole again.

The church is understood as the first sprouts of this new garden, the liturgy as the nurturing of the Spirit's emerging life. In order that all the people be made whole, God begins with this community. For all the created order to be sanctified, God begins with this bread and wine. Classically called the epiclesis, one part of the great thanksgiving invokes the Spirit upon the bread and wine, that the new creation can be signified by this transformed food. As the food, so we: The Spirit is invoked upon the community, and finally upon the whole earth, that not merely this small meal but the entire created order will manifest the resurrection.

But despite the church's imagery of a dove descending and fire alighting, in real life sanctification cannot always be seen with the eye. The Spirit comes upon the bread; the infant is baptized. Do we see any holiness? Sometimes yes, sometimes no. When we long to listen to the choirs of white-robed martyrs, we hear instead a parish committee rattling around like Ezekiel's valley of dry bones. So we continue praying: *Veni, Creator Spiritus.*

Ezekiel 37:1–14

Grain once scattered on the hillsides,
sanctify, O Spirit of God,
into a heavenly loaf.
Bones now strewn dry in the valley,
sanctify, O Spirit of God,
into a living body.
We are each one separated:
O Holy One,
breathe us whole.

Body and Blood of Christ

Through the centuries, by the thousands, Christians assemble each Sunday to give thanks for the presence of Christ in their midst. Following the pattern of Jewish praise, Christians recite before God the historic events in which they have seen this saving divine presence. Thus at each eucharist we retell the story of Jesus' last supper with his disciples before his death, seeing in this event and in Jesus' odd words a paradigm of God's salvation.

The words of Jesus at the last supper have come down to us in several different Greek formulations. The church has translated the sacred words something like this: "This is my body, this is the cup of the new covenant in my blood." It is unlikely that Jesus spoke Greek, and his Aramaic, which did not allow for this particular use of the verb "to be," could not say precisely the four words "This is my body." But it is the Greek phrases that inspire our praise, that we translate into English, that we cite at the center of our thanksgiving.

Indeed, over these enigmatic words considerably many heads have rolled. As medieval Europe focused social authority ever more univocally in the church, and the church's authority in the priesthood, it is no wonder that a certain set of words by which the priest claimed to make God present usurped attention away from the people's praise. The Latin words *Hoc est enim corpus meum* were popularly misunderstood as a magical formula, from which derives our word hocus-pocus. It is also no surprise that our century's renewed appreciation for the assembled people of God has meant less theological intensity over these sacred words. But while we no longer burn one another at the stake over philosophical categories, we continue to probe the meaning of these words. How is Christ present in our midst?

The New Testament itself suggests several different ways to think about the bread and wine as the real presence of Christ in our midst. Luke, true to his historical bent as a narrator of the life of Christ and the course of the church, tells about Jesus' meals with his disciples. Luke writes of the miraculous feeding of the crowds on the hillside, of Jesus' dinner with Zacchaeus, of Jesus' last supper before his death, of the disciples' meals with the resurrected Lord, and of the community's meals after the ascension. When on Easter Day Jesus eats with the two disciples at Emmaus, Jesus "took the bread and blessed, and broke it, and gave it to them." The two disciples appeared not to have understood Jesus' sermon on the road, but they do know him in their midst at the breaking of the bread.

Luke 9:12–17
Luke 19:2–10
Luke 22:7–23
Luke 24:13–43
Acts 2:46
Luke 24:30

Paul the theologian is not so interested in all the stories of Jesus. Rather than giving narrative details, he writes that the crucifixion is the meaning of the last supper, that the crucifixion is the meaning of the community's meal together. Christ is in our midst when as the community of the body of Christ we gather around his death, remember his death, and live out his death in our communal life. To eat in a worthy way, we are to discern the body; that is, we are to recognize this community around the bread and wine as the body of Christ in the world.

1 Corinthians 11:26

It was for John, the master of metaphor, to describe the presence of Christ as the believers' ingesting the life of God in the bread and wine. The Johannine community understood that Christ is present when we take Christ into ourselves, as the Son has been taken into the Father. As the food is in us, so the Son is in us; as the Son is in us, so the Son is in the Father; as the bread and wine are in us, so we are in God.

John 6:35–51

These different biblical emphases inspired theologians to try their own hand. In *The Mysteries*, Ambrose, declaring that the bread is now the body of Christ, writes "Why do we use arguments? Let us use Christ's own examples," says Ambrose the typologist. Moses's rod becomes a serpent; the rivers of Egypt flow blood; the Jordan River parts for the Israelites; water pours out from the rock. The grace of God is able to work contrary to nature: Think of the virgin birth, Ambrose says. This eucharistic food is like the apples on the tree in the beloved's garden, like manna raining from heaven. The biblical images of saving grace become images of the bread and wine of the eucharist.

Similarly, in his *Lectures on the Christian Sacraments*, Cyril of Jerusalem cites the miracle of the water turned to wine. The bread and wine, writes Cyril, are "the figures" of the body and blood of Christ. The bread and wine now bear Christ, and we too, when eating the bread and wine, come also to bear Christ. We becomes Christophers, says Cyril: What happens to the bread and wine happens also to us.

Augustine uses the idea of the real presence to teach the unity of the church. We receive the presence of Christ by faith. As well, by faith in God's grace this body of Christ makes us to be what we are: the body of Christ. "You are what you have received," reads Augustine's Easter sermon 227. In Pentecost's sermon 272, Augustine preaches, "If you are the body of Christ and his members, it is your mystery which has been placed on the altar of the Lord; you receive your own mystery." The mystery of the bread and wine becoming body and blood is one with the mystery of countless Christian assemblies becoming the single body of Christ.

In early medieval times a literalism became popular. By the eleventh century a dissident theologian had to sign a statement affirming that the body of Christ was literally torn by his teeth. Priests felt compelled to confess their anguish at tasting not blood but wine. Clearly the explanatory language was inadequate, and debates began to rage.

Scholasticism proposed a brilliant solution to this philosophical dilemma. With Aristotle's theories about reality being
an amalgam of substance and accidents, Thomas Aquinas was
able to suggest that although the accidents remained the same—
one's teeth did not tear at Christ's flesh—the substance
changed. The substance was what a thing really was. Aquinas
wrote that were a mouse to eat the consecrated bread, the mouse
would not receive the substance of Christ's body. For the mouse
had not the faith to receive the substance that the church in
faith received.

By the fifteenth century a new philosophical theory
rejected Aristotle's dual description of reality, and thus the
Reformers reverted to Augustine's teachings on faith without the
assistance of Thomism. Luther remained adamant that Christ
was really present in the sacrament, and when angered by more
radical Protestant views that the bread and wine only symbolized
Christ's body and blood, Luther responded with religious paradox: The meal was both bread and body, both wine and blood.
We see his stress on the real presence in a seldom-quoted treatise
written against the "enthusiastic" radical Reformers, "Before I
would have mere wine with the enthusiasts, I would take only
blood with the Pope" (Weimar 26:462). So the debates continue
to rage.

Sometimes during debate, contemporary Christians pretend
to be their founders. It is easier to repeat the speeches of fourth-
century preachers or thirteenth-century philosophers or
sixteenth-century reformers than it is to think anew, and so all
too often current conversation sounds like the lines in a bad
historical play. But some among us are continuing the Western
task of trying to say what the words mean. Several Dutch

theologians—P. Schooneberg and E. Schillebeeckx—are articulating how modern philosophy and psychology describe reality and determine meaning. "Transsignification" is one suggestion for how we are to think of the body and blood of Christ as really present. It is by communal agreement on meaning that the human community grants to anything its reality, and in the eucharist the meaning of the bread has been changed from bread to body. The meal is about how the assembled community encounters Christ.

Not only the philosophy of theologians, but also the metaphors of poets have been inspired by these phrases from the last supper. In her *Revelations of Divine Love,* Julian of Norwich sees the food of the eucharist as the milk from the breasts of her mother Jesus. In her prayer of February 16, 1379, Catherine of Siena addresses God as table and food and waiter, the Father being the table who presents the Son as food and the Spirit being the waiter who feeds us on our way. Thomas Aquinas, in a stanza inexplicably suppressed in modern translations of *"Adoro te devote,"* sees the blood of Christ in the eucharist as the life-blood the mother pelican pours out from her breast to save her dying offspring. In the seventeenth-century eucharistic hymn "Soul, adorn yourself with gladness," Johann Franck employs the age-old image of marriage: We receive the food as the joyous lover receives the beloved.

Here is yet another way to explicate the sacred words "This is my body, this is the cup of the new covenant in my blood." These words spoken in their context are an icon for the Trinity. It is almighty God whom we seek, whose presence we hunger and thirst for. In the life and deeds—yes, the body—of Jesus of Nazareth, we encounter that God. God calls us to the table and feeds us with food made possible only because of the death of

Jesus, God's Son. For God could not eat with us were God the immortal essence of Greek philosophy. In Jesus the incarnate God is among us.

But "This is my body" means just as fully that in the gathered community is the Spirit of that Son. We, this community, this body of Christ, are the mystery of the Son of God in the midst of the world. We see the Spirit of God not in some puff of cloud hovering near the sun in the sky; we see that Spirit in the eyes and palms and lips of the faithful who come forward to eat and to drink. In the bread is the body of the Son, in the eating of the bread is the Spirit of God.

Drink! We have not said enough about drink. It makes sense to see bread as sustenance from the creator, as the staple of life. But wine is more and other than food: It is festival, fun, delight, joy. It requires human creativity and human time. It is communal drink. It can be misused by the lonely, dismissed by the dour. And even in this century of sophisticated medical knowlege, wine in one cup has frightened us with its powerful symbolism of shared life. But we all are invited to drink up: not solely the priest, not by the plastic thimbleful, but poured out and shared by the community, which is itself the mystery.

O God,
creator of seed and vine,
farmer and vintner supreme,
here is your mystery:
Jesus your body,
we your body,
drinking our way into your dominion.

Father

Here we are finally at a controversial word. Although most of the liturgy's words have layers of meaning and variations of usage, in Father we have a real fight on our hands—sheep and goats butting and biting each other, both sides of the tug-of-war convinced that only in their place is the liberating gospel. Some of the people who hail from my conservative Lutheran upbringing judge it heretical even to reduce the occurrences of the name Father; some of my feminist friends refuse to pronounce it; many of us say Father with only half our mouth. It is shaky to publish opinions on this word, for the mind of the church keeps shifting, not sure of stable ground, wondering whether the solid rock is where it used to be.

Of course, as now almost everyone is quick to note, Father is in some ways the wrong word. The word in Paul's letters and in Mark's gospel is Abba, a word that seems to have been important to Jesus, a familial title of affection and endearment, a different image from God as heavenly father of the king, a symbol that Christianity inherited from the patriarchal monarchies of the ancient Near East. Psalm 89 says that King David is the son of the Father, but the psalmist does not call God Abba. Yet scholars now theorize that Abba was not a title unique to Jesus and Abba is not a child's term, as Aramaic scholars conjectured earlier in this century. Shall we even use the word Father to translate the opening line of the Lord's Prayer?

Romans 8:15–16

Mark 14:36

We ought not be surprised by the inadequacy of our word. There has always been similar difficulty in translating El Shaddai, the name of God disclosed to Abram. Almighty God, the tradition has rendered it, already in the Greek not even attempting actually to translate Shaddai. The goddess's breasts or the god's mountaintops, hinted at by the term Shaddai, are dismissed by the easy abstraction Almighty. Naming

Genesis 17:1

God is hard enough; translating the names into ever-changing languages is proving to be nigh impossible.

We pray the Our Father because our tradition labels it the prayer Jesus taught. Scholars remind us that the petitions are not unique to Jesus or his movement. For the most part the prayer sounds like the plea of any first-century Palestinian Jew who awaited the coming of the dominion of God. Yet biblical tradition gives us these particular words—gives us, in fact, the two different versions of them in Matthew and Luke—as the prayer taught by Jesus. Furthermore, church tradition claims that we can share Jesus' words because through baptism we share in his intimate relationship with God. Tradition urges us to repeat the Our Father as our primary prayer.

Matthew 6:9–13
Luke 11:2–4

But, of course, tradition is a living thing. Tradition is not like an obsolete edition of the encyclopedia, full of half-facts and old prejudices. Tradition is not like a 1948 etiquette book that lists the activities and even the fabrics forbidden a widow in deep mourning. In contrast, the tradition of the church lives. We can read medieval books long dismissed, we can unearth attitudes that were subsequently buried, we can make tradition different tomorrow than it was yesterday or today. Although we cannot dismiss the prejudice against laywomen in medieval times, that we now read the adventures of Margery Kempe changes for us our sense of the church in the fourteenth and fifteenth centuries. And where would liturgists be had Egeria's diary never come to light? When "tradition" repeats tired slogans out of context, when "tradition" yells louder and louder to drown out queries, it becomes a sarcophagus that the dying church deserves. But when tradition is the history of the movement of the Spirit, darting here, birthing there, migrating halfway around the world, it can serve as one expression of

God's truth. On the word "Father," we quickly discover that our tradition had the word too small.

OUR FATHER IN HEAVEN. The immediate image in the Western imagination is all too predictable. Up on the mountaintop, or floating somewhere between earth and sky, or located outside the universe beyond the music of the spheres is a glorious land which is home to the divine *paterfamilias*. Our own human experience of family is writ large over the universe: A father, either autocratic or gracious, dispenses discipline or favor. It is a simple and in some ways a meager image through which faith travels to deeper attempts to picture grace.

In the fourth century we find one such deeper attempt. When lecturing to newly baptized adults, Cyril of Jerusalem explicated the meaning of the Lord's Prayer. For him, Father was a positive word because it offered a contrast to the current image of God as the alien and ruthless monarch of the world—not a big problem in contemporary consciousness. Of the opening to the prayer Cyril says something brilliant. Describing "in heaven" he writes: "They, too, are a heaven who bear the image of the heavenly, in whom God is, dwelling and walking in them." Heaven is not only an imaginative layer outside the stratosphere, a religious idea about the abode of the Almighty: Heaven is this assembly, for here in these believers God dwells. We meet the God whom we address, not out there, but here, in the Spirit of this praying congregation.

YOUR KINGDOM COME. Here another age-old religious stereotype clicks in. Many are the religions which describe divinity as a great monarch, usually a king, sometimes a queen, sometimes a royal couple, sitting on gem-studded thrones just as they sit on the poor and oppressed people. Their crowns are a nimbus of brilliant light turned into gleaming gold, their scepters are oppressors' rods in bejeweled camouflage. Perhaps the myths tell of a benevolent dictatorship. But even then the rituals have much to do with elaborate techniques of how to gain an audience with the mighty and fearful sovereign. We must learn how to court favor, how to construct acceptable petitions, how to offer appropriate gifts. Christianity contracted some of this after the peace of Constantine when the emperor was no longer a threat but a patron: Vestments came to resemble royal robes, and liturgical vessels looked like treasure chests in a glorious glut of ostentation.

But for a procession with the relic of the cross that took place on November 19, 568, Venantius Honorius Fortunatus provided a hymn that summons us out of the throne room. The royal banners, *vexilla regis,* lead the triumphal march of the king of glory. The poem demonstrates that the poet knew all the classic imagery to celebrate monarchy. Yet the throne from which this God reigns is a tree, its boughs made crimson with the red of blood. And not Fortunatus alone, but many other poets and hymn writers, the anonymous Anglo-Saxon author of *The Dream of the Rood* among them, remind us of a truth that requires the paradox of poetry to express: The kingdom we anticipate is ruled by the man dying on the cross. "Behold your king!" calls out

John 19:14 Pilate of his prisoner. We are the thief on the cross, and Jesus promises us entry into his kingdom today. But what kind of kingdom? Surely not one of dazzling gold. This dominion glows with the light of Christ, which contains the Good Friday darkness and the night of the grave. Thus we meet the God whom we address, not only in the Spirit of this assembly but also enthroned on the Good Friday cross.

GIVE US TODAY OUR DAILY BREAD. We have seen deeper into Father and King, but there is yet another religious stereotype to limit our prayer. Our prayer for food can sound like every other cry for bread. How many billions of petitioners have approached the Creator to plead for food? How often have we clamored for the Creator's attention? Just a little more creation, for me this time, we beg: today's food, tomorrow's life. In his catechism, Martin Luther taught that this petition includes our plea for all the good things of life, "everything that belongs to the support and wants of the body," and his list included "a pious spouse, pious children, pious servants, good friends, faithful neighbors, and the like." Oh, that the beneficent Creator will keep on creating, bringing forth bread from the earth, for me, so faithfully praying! But translators agree that the Greek word for "daily" does not really mean "daily." This is not a typical religious cry for today's meal. Indeed, we have come to expect that Christian words mean more, if not other, than their surface definition.

A woman who knew this in the fourteenth century lived in a hut attached to a church in Norwich, England. We know her as Julian, although since the church was St. Julian, that may not be her baptized name at all. She wrote in her *Revelations of Divine Love* that it is our tender mother Jesus who feeds us. Our Lord, Julian envisioned, "our natural mother, our gracious mother," bears us in joy, feeds us with himself, and cares for us most tenderly. Not some abstract Creator, a philosophically acceptable Prime Mover of the seasons and harvests, but the God that we know in Jesus feeds us with extraordinary bread. All the bread we consume, all the food we require, comes from the life of this Mother. I am the bread from heaven, I am the water you crave, you must be born again, say the paradoxes of John's gospel.

I do not know why Jesus addressed God as Abba. We can know extremely little about the mind of Jesus; we can only guess from what the evangelists imply, what Paul teaches, what first-century records intimate. Perhaps we would be better served these days to open the prayer as Jesus did, with "Abba." As with the words Christ, Amen, Hosanna and Hallelujah, the original language transliterated may be better than an inadequate translation. But I am helped by the old Latin cue line, *audemus dicere,* "we are bold to say." I need such boldness to pray so outrageously, a feminist to a middle-aged man's fatherly God. But then I need such boldness to pray at all, when so much of the language of faith seems unsatisfactory before faith's magnificent visions and inadequate to the world's unending miseries. I wonder: What does it mean to pray in a tradition in which there are so many words I would never myself choose?

But while I am struggling, here comes the Lord's Prayer again. And when the assembly prays together, we find ourselves standing before the Trinity. God is more than what we first believed: God is the Spirit of this assembly, God is in Jesus on the cross, God is the nurturing mother of our life. I am grateful for the faithful poets: The very tradition before which I balk offers me also other folk who struggled with holy words: Cyril and Fortunatus and Julian. I like to think of them helping me learn how to pray.

A ba ba ba, receive our babble,
syllables crying out for God and life and food,
that we may live.
A ba ba ba, teach us to pray.

Peace

"Peace," we say to others in the pew, alongside, in front, in back. "Peace," we say, and if you are my age perhaps you think of Woodstock, middle-class American kids costumed in cast-off clothing, ten strands of beads and daisy chains, singing antiwar ballads. If you are older perhaps you recall the footage shown each June 6 on public television stations, the film record of the forces landing in Normandy, all the Allied soldiers running straight into enemy fire, finally the power of good making inroads against the forces of evil. Perhaps my daughters think of department stores selling pieces of the Berlin Wall. But let us see about deepening and widening our images of peace: What does scripture tell us about "the peace of the Lord"?

Our first reading is the story of Gideon's call, told in the sixth chapter of the Book of Judges. The Israelite tribes are being *Judges 6:11–24* harassed by the Midianite tribes, and Israel's young life as an agricultural settlement is threatened. The angel of the LORD appears to Gideon, calling him to lead the Israelite tribes to victory. Gideon, aware of his own weakness and the people's vulnerability, seeks assurance. Employing an ancient religious ritual, he sets out sacrificial food—meat, matzos, broth—and the angel, miraculously evoking fire from the rock, consumes the food. Now believing that the messenger has come from the LORD, Gideon accepts the commission, but he fears this God more than he fears the Midianites. In a surprising turn of the story, the LORD says to Gideon, "Peace be to you." Gideon erects an altar there and calls the shrine "The LORD is peace."

Martin Luther would call this narrative "gospel." The people are suffering under social disorientation and military oppression; they are gearing up to intensify the warfare; Israelite identity in the promised land may never be realized. After all, even Gideon's own father worships the Canaanite deities, the goddess Asherah and the god Baal. But into this human mess comes an angel of God with the good news that the LORD is peace. The LORD who is peace will bring peace: peace for the Israelite tribes; peace between Gideon and his father, even after Gideon knocks down his father's sacred pole and holy bull; peace between terrified humankind and the mighty God. The LORD brings peace: God will save.

Judges 6:25–27

Our psalm is 122, a hymn sung by the Hebrew pilgrims upon arriving at the temple in Jerusalem. The city, the home of the king, has become a symbol of the strength and unity and security of the people, a sign to them of God's blessings in this promised land. The city manifests an end to war and fragmentation. In the city is the house of the LORD, the sign of God's presence, creating the condition for peace. Peace be within the city and with all its people, the poet sings.

Ephesians 2:11–22

Our second reading is from Ephesians 2. The human problem is again understood as social and religious fragmentation. We are separated from God; Jews and Greeks are pitted against one another; people are feeling like nomads again; all are treated like strangers; all seek oneness with God. The Christian response to this perennial problem is Christ: Christ is our peace, Christ breaks down walls, Christ is the cornerstone of one grand temple in which all live peacefully in the Spirit of God. Do you seek the strength and unity and security of the citadel of Jerusalem? Here is the church of Christ, says the writer of Ephesians. Here is the Spirit, here the Lord's peace.

John 20:19–29

Our gospel reading is from John 20. Only a woman has seen the risen Lord, and first-century men did not grant women enough credence to allow them to testify in court. But on the first day of the week, and then again eight days later, yet again on the first day of the week, the risen Lord appears within the assembly of the disciples. They too feel embattled: They know disintegration of their dreams, terror for their own safety, confusion about life's meaning. But here is Christ in their midst, bidding them peace. Gideon sees fire burst from a rock; the pilgrims see the shining gates of the holy city; and in this, the climax of John's gospel, Thomas sees Jesus and cries out, "My Lord and my God."

In this exclamation Thomas means not only that before him stands his earthly master, the leader of his religious group. "Lord" in the Greek has a double meaning. It signifies both our word "sir," the common form of address to the male authority, and the sacred name of God, the YHWH of the burning bush. Here is the primordial Christian confession: This risen Jesus is the living God among us. Into our weekly assembly comes the resurrected Christ who is God bringing peace.

With these biblical texts ringing "peace" in our ears, we come to the *Pax vobiscum*. Decades of Victorian manners may suggest that "peace" is about inner contentment, about patience and resignation, about subdued conversation rather than boisterous argumentation. I remember the song we sang in Girl Scouts:

> Peace, I ask of thee, O river,
> Peace, peace, peace.
> When I learn to live serenely,
> Cares will cease.

The words are not only flagrantly erroneous; they are not a helpful model for the *Pax vobiscum*. The peace of the Lord must be other than a preference for mellow personality types.

In Latin, of course, the plural is obvious. Peace comes in the assembly when Christ is in our midst. Peace is promised to

the Israelite tribes, peace is typified by the city, the peace of
Christ brings all the disparate folk into one whole new being.
The peace of Christian individuals is a communal confession of
the power of the Spirit—an experience not likely to mellow us
out in contentment. "The LORD is peace," acclaimed Gideon,

Judges 7–8

and strode off to bloody battle. "The peace of the Lord," said the
first Christians to one another, and Ananias and Sapphira get

Acts 5:1–11

struck down dead for lying about their church contributions.

Thomas Aquinas taught that the language we use about
God has its primary meaning in its religious context. That is, to
understand the phrase "God is judge," we look to the scriptures'
depictions of God's judging; only later do we compare this meaning to the secular meaning of "judge." If mishandled, this
suggestion of Aquinas merely provides us a way to weasel out of
inadequate translations. But in understanding the peace,
Aquinas is helpful. We cannot begin with images of Woodstock
or the Normandy invasion or contentment by the river, for there
is no evidence that Christians are granted the kind of peace for
which the world strives. What was that about Jesus bringing not

Matthew 10:34

peace but a sword?

Rather it is as if "peace" is yet another metaphor for God.
How do we say "the presence of God among us"? We say peace.
To define the word, we inquire into the evidence of God's presence among us. The Hebrew Scriptures speak of *shalom*, the
fullness of life. The people of Israel tell of the road to freedom,
the New Testament of resurrection; both are ways to speak of
new life. The new life of God's Spirit, enlivening the community: Who knows where this peace will burst bonds apart, when
this peace will shatter the tomb's door? What must make way for
there to be room for God's fullness?

Some Christian communities, introducing the exchange of peace, outsmarted themselves. It's only a regular old handshake, we said, to encourage ease in the new ritual. In some assemblies now everyone must greet everyone, checking on the week's calendar and the days' news. In yet other communities, a wooden handshake is nailed in place, as folk reared to private devotion let one other person into their cell for the moment.

I do not mean to suggest that the ritual be highly formalized, the presider's left hand on the altar, the Lord's peace carefully passed down the pews from the holy place to the back seat. But I do mean to remember the fire bursting from the rock, the glorious city and the wounds of the risen Lord. I do mean to urge that sharing the peace is not merely a hello to the friend, not only the greeting to the stranger. It is the end of invading tribes, the security of the monarchical capital, the reconciliation of ancient enemies. The slaves escape; the dead are raised. The primordial barriers between human and divine are torn down; as the Exsultet says, earth and heaven are wed. Yes, the peace of Christ is in the community, human life recreated by the presence of God.

Grant us peace
Be our peace
peace and your wounds
peace and a sword
the peace of your presence
which is beyond our peace
peace beyond our understanding.

Mercy

One of the insights popularized by contemporary feminists concerns the word "mercy." They have reminded the church that the Hebrew word that Christians have translated "mercy" is the plural of the Hebrew word for womb. Thus exegetes and poets and catechists are now reveling in this linguistic surprise, the truth of which was known to the faithful throughout the ages: that God's mercy is a nurturing womb, that we are enlivened by the embracing life of God, that our life is borne from God, that our sustenance comes through God, that we crowd together— siblings on top of one another—in that dark and watery birthplace filled to overflowing with mercy. God's mercy, like a father's arms, a mother's belly, upholds us all who like infants are wholly dependent on our parents, *abba* and *imma*, for life.

So it is that God's mercy is a bountiful womb for us. The rabbis, wishing to incorporate into their synagogue liturgy the passage from Exodus 34—"The Lord, a God merciful and gracious, slow to anger, and abounding in steadfast love and faithfulness"—were surprised at the next line, that God "will by no means clear the guilty." Their communal faith and their liturgical formation was in a God more merciful than this negative phrase suggested. Thus, the rabbis decided to include the Exodus passage in their liturgy, but with the negative deleted. They believed God would indeed clear the guilty. And so the faithful always search for metaphors and images of so great a mercy. As the Maronite Christians pray at the close of their eucharistic prayer, "When placed on a scale, your mercy prevails over the weight of the mountains known only to you."

Yes, we now more easily equate mercy with womb, hoping to counterbalance Michelangelo's big man in the sky with God's mothering care. But words always wriggle away from our definitions, behind our backs capturing other meanings, being caught

Exodus 34:6–7

by alien connotations. The metaphor of maternal womb is not great enough to contain our experience of God's mercy.

The womb is the abode of human life perpetually in need of mercy, and this human need pleading for divine mercy pervades the scriptures. The world is in peril, society in shambles, our bodies infirm, our guilt overwhelming—and we plead for

Jonah 1–4

mercy. The story of Jonah illustrates this divine mercy. God rescues the runaway Jonah by sending a fish to save him from drowning. God forgives the Ninevites when they repent in dust and ashes. And when Jonah sits pouting outside the city walls, grousing about the too-easy mercy of God, God calls also Jonah to mercy for all the thousands of pitiful people, and—as the last phrase of the story says—mercy for even the cattle.

One of our mothers in mercy, Hannah, had often cried out

1 Samuel 1

in need. She was barren, and in a culture which measured a woman's worth by the number of her sons, she lived shamed by the community, ridiculed by her husband's other wife, unaided by God. So she prays at the shrine for a son, prays so fervently that the old priest scolds her incoherence. Hannah becomes yet another Hebrew woman who conceives a child with the help of God, and when she delivers her son Samuel to the shrine to be apprenticed to the holy things, she sings praises to God's mercy

1 Samuel 2:1–10

Luke 2:46–55

for turning the world upside-down to favor the needy.

A millennium later, Mary also sings God's praises. She sees that the raising of the poor and the humbling of the mighty are signs of God's mercy, the mercy promised to all the chosen people from Abraham to the end of time. Yet it is not only childbearing women who praise God's mercy. In the Gospels of Matthew, Mark and Luke, it is the sick who beg for mercy. The

Matthew 15:22

Matthew 17:15

mother of the mad daughter, the father of the epileptic son, the

ten lepers, and in all three gospels the blind, cry out, *"Eleison* *Luke 17:13*
Mark 10:47

me, eleison hemas," "Have mercy on me, have mercy on us."

With a cry for mercy the liturgy begins, in the litany of
"Lord, have mercy." With a cry for mercy the service of the word
concludes, as we pray for all the world's needy. With a cry for
mercy we assemble at the table to claim the bread broken for us.
"Mercy," we cry at the beginning, middle and end. Mercy is the
womb we enter when we worship together. I think of the pil-
grimage church at the monastery of Taizé, France: While all our
home churches are busy repainting walls gleaming white and
installing powerful light fixtures and designing spaces of bright-
ness, the Taizé church embraces us with a merciful round
darkness. It is too dark to read, but we are encircled with votive
lights as with a palpable mercy. All the pilgrims, all the languages, all the denominations, all the ages sit there on the unlit
floor, themselves walking bodies of need, settled now into divine
compassion, in, under, around, through.

We cry mercy as we gather around the table for the bread
and wine; mercy, as the bread is broken; mercy, as friend and
stranger commune; mercy also for me. But this is not like private
confession and absolution, in which the word comes specifically
to me. This mercy is for all, and for me as part of the all. The
body of Christ "for you" is a plural you, you all, not the "for you,
Suzie" that one hears these days. The table trains us in the habit
of mercy by serving up mercy to all equally, each one of us —
whether we know it or not — as needy as the next. Communion
ought to train us to such mercy even when the table has been
cleared, mercy we now are to share with one another through
the week.

Mercy: I think of two fifteenth-century paintings by Giovanni Bellini. One is a Pietá that cries mercy in every detail. An old Mary with heavily lined face holds the dead Jesus, his legs fallen over her knees, his arms hanging down, with fifteenth-century Ravenna in the background. Through the realism of an old grieving woman and a crucified Christ outside a contemporaneous city, the painting speaks of God's present mercy to the needy. Thirty years earlier, Bellini had painted a much more symbolic piece: The beautiful virgin, crowned with a halo, is seated on a gold throne suspended in the sky. But the infant on her lap rests with his legs fallen over her knees and his arm hanging down as only a dead adult could lie. So here too in the Madonna and Child is God's mercy, the compassion of the crucifixion in the image of the incarnation. It is as if the Madonna and Child taught Bellini about the mercy of the Pietá, just as the liturgy can teach us the mercy we evidence many years later.

Mercy: It seems that my fourth-grade parochial teacher informed us that if we died while sinning, we would go to hell. Dutiful as I was, and gullible to boot, I went home quite afraid and did not sleep all night, frantic that I would dream an evil thought, die, and wake up in everlasting damnation. The truth is, however, that I don't remember this part of the adventure. What I recall is that the next morning at six o'clock my father phoned my teacher and railed at him for terrorizing students with the heresy that the sin of a baptized child could be greater than the mercy of God.

We teach God's mercy to our children, and we write *Deuteronomy 6:9* "mercy" on the doorposts of our heart, and we frame our eucharist with pleas for mercy. It is good to learn how to pronounce the word, for there will come a time for each of us—unless we die as very young children—to make use of that word. For each of us comes the year, or the day, or the moment, when all the blood is seeping out, when the cord is wrapped around our neck, when what we hoped would be life is rather death, death, death. Then we need to know the cry for mercy, the exchange of our womb of human life gone dead for the womb of God. In that womb, we are free even to die: For there we will be safe, dead or alive, in the mercy of God.

O God whose name is mercy,
we are barren: Have mercy!
We are blind: Have mercy!
Feed us through the walls of your womb.
By the birth of your Son,
by the death of your Son,
have mercy on us,
now and at the hour of our death.

Amen

A simple Amen at the end.

After so many words—spoken, sung, read, preached, heard—there is a final Amen. After all our efforts to render God's mercy in contemporary American English, we revert to ancient Hebrew, bonding ourselves with those who millenia ago stood together and in one voice shouted their Amen. This word has always had significance for Christians: We discover in Paul's letters that Greek-speaking Christians called out this ancient Jewish acclamation when they spoke their Christian prayers, believing that through Christ, God was their every end, their every beginning.

2 Corinthians 1:20

Revelation 22:13

Because we customarily conclude our prayers with Amen, some folk think the word is final punctuation, a Yup-now-it's-over sound. Actually the opposite is more true. The word calls us into the future of the words just heard. The liturgy's words of praise and petition are by no means over. The Sunday hour has placed them at the outset of the week, and the final Amen is our way to claim those words in ourselves for the coming seven days. Amen, yes, so it is, so it will be.

In a black Baptist church, the preacher was warming up, talking gently in the first minutes of the sermon. From a back pew one of the Mothers called out, "Amen! Preach it, Brother!" Her Amen was to cheer him on, to get him going in his task, to begin the praises. When the minister gives us the bread and the cup, saying, "The body of Christ, the blood of Christ," we call out Amen: not because the event is now over, but because it is now beginning again, we take into our community the life of God. Amen, we say: Yes, let it begin.

You all know that magnificent passage from the Book of Revelation, the poem the reader chokes up on in Year C on Good Shepherd Sunday. All the saints and all the people from

Revelation 7:9–17

every language and tribe and nation are gathered around the throne and the Lamb. It is the time of no more hunger, no more tears: There is living water for everyone. In the temple all the angels and the four creatures and the elders lead the hymn of praise: "Amen! Blessing and glory and wisdom and thanksgiving and honor and power and might be to our God for ever and ever! Amen!" Their praise concludes with an Amen as it began with an Amen. For the praise is never over, but begins always again.